The Actor's Mirror

Reclaiming Realism in an Age of Simulation

The Screen Actor's Guide to Truth and Transformation

by Adam Smith Jr.

The Actor's Mirror
Reclaiming Realism in an Age of Simulation

Copyright © 2025 by Adam Smith Jr.
All rights reserved.

Originally registered under the working title:
Throw It Away — And Mean It

No part of this book may be reproduced, stored in a retrieval system, or transmitted in any form or by any means—electronic, mechanical, photocopying, recording, or otherwise—without the prior written permission of the publisher, except for brief quotations used in reviews or scholarly analysis.

U.S. Copyright Registration No. 1-14921652671

For information or permissions, contact:
adam@thebrownstoneclass.com

ISBN: 979-8-218-68604-8

Published by Brownstone Books

Foreword

As a theatre scholar, acting teacher, and performer, I have spent decades steeped in the philosophies of performance. Rarely have I encountered a book as urgent, clear-eyed, and necessary as that of *The Actor's Mirror: Reclaiming Realism in an Age of Simulation*. Adam Smith Jr. has not simply written a book on acting; he has issued a call to arms.

This work is part diagnosis, part rebellion, and wholly alive. In an era when performances can be simulated, faces deepfaked, and spontaneity surgically replaced by post-production trickery, Smith dares to assert that the human actor *still* matters. He demands that we remember what acting is *for*—not to showcase reality but to hold the mirror to nature, as Hamlet demanded, and *choose where to aim it*.

Smith's central insight—that our training methods have collapsed realism into naturalism—is not merely an academic point. It's a deep-rooted problem that permeates into performance, pedagogy, and the actor's sense of self. This book offers a lifeline to those who have felt stuck in hollow "truthfulness," in studios obsessed with emotional recall, or on sets that replace collaborators with tennis balls and green screens. Here, realism is not restraint—it is revelation. It's not about being smaller for the camera; it's about being honest in front of it.

Like Boleslavsky's *Acting: The First Six Lessons* over a century ago, what I find so extraordinary about *The Actor's Mirror* is Smith's marriage of fierce intellectual clarity with real-world compassion. He writes with the authority of a scholar, the eye of a working actor, and the heart of a teacher who has sat across from the uncertain, the burned out, and the brave. His exercises are not theoretical—they are kinetic, grounded, and often thrilling. His chapters trace a lineage of actors and thinkers who've wrestled with the craft—from Stella Adler's expansive vision to Michael Chekhov's imaginative precision—yet Smith's voice remains uniquely his own: *urgent, alive, unpretentious*.

If you are an actor tired of "just be real" as instruction...
If you are a teacher weary of passing down inherited methods that no longer serve your students...
If you are a director, casting agent, or audience member craving performances that do not vanish into imitation but vibrate with *meaning*—
This book is for you.

In *The Actor's Mirror*, Smith reminds us that acting is not self-disclosure, but self-transcendence. Not mimicry, but a deliberate, physical, and philosophical act of imagination. It is not about vanishing into the role—it is about wielding the performance as a site of confrontation, transformation, and yes, sometimes even revolution.

In these pages, you won't find DIY prescriptions or nostalgia for golden ages. You'll find a rigorous, embodied, imaginative practice for actors who *want* to matter in an age that increasingly prefers simulation over soul.

Read it. Teach it. Use it.

Aaron Adair, Ph.D.

Table Of Contents

The Actor's Mirror 1

Foreword 3

Table Of Contents 5

Introduction: This Is a Revolution 7

Chapter One: Not a Day Like Any Other 11

Chapter Two: Out of The Cave 22

Chapter Three: The Meaning of Realism 30

Chapter Four: The Group Theatre's Beautiful Mistake 38

Chapter Five: Strasberg and the Tyranny of the Inner Life 46

Chapter Six: What Stella Knew 54

Chapter Eight: The Art of Seeing 70

Chapter Nine: Preparation for Collision 76

Chapter Ten: Prepare for Anything 82

Chapter Eleven: Lines, Lines, Lines 88

Chapter Twelve: The Power of Why 96

The Brownstone Script Analysis Tool 103

Chapter Thirteen: Action Without Stakes Is Dead 109

Chapter Fourteen: A New Pedagogy — Philosophy, Imagination, and the Body 117

Chapter Fifteen: The Actor's Responsibility 124

Chapter Sixteen: A Tale of Two Tightropes 130

Chapter Seventeen: To Action — To Throw It Away and Mean It 137

Chapter Eighteen: Take After Take 143

Chapter Nineteen: Acting as Sport 149

Chapter Twenty: The Lineage of Liberation 158

Epilogue: The Last Undeniable Thing — Acting in a Manufactured World 163

Final Chapter: Hating the Waiting — Resilience in the Age of Delay 167

Acknowledgments 173

Glossary of Terms 174

About the Author 179

Introduction: This Is a Revolution

I didn't set out to write a book. I set out to fix something.

Modern actor training—especially for the screen—is broken. It still clings to the rituals and rules of a different era. It worships naturalism without question. It fetishizes emotional recall. It trains actors to look inward and dig into personal wounds instead of building the world of the story. It teaches them to shrink—when what the camera demands is not restraint, but truth.

But now the problem is bigger.

We've entered an era where human performance is no longer a given. Where deepfake actors read cue cards with perfect subtlety. Where AI reanimates the dead to sell us things. Where a scene partner might be a tennis ball on a C-stand in front of a green screen—because the real scene, the real partner, the real story will be stitched in later. The industry calls it "efficiency." I call it erasure.

Naturalism—the surface appearance of being real—has become cheap. Algorithms can replicate it. Studios can simulate it. A computer can approximate human behavior better than many actors trained only to imitate life.

If we train actors only to imitate, we are training them into obsolescence.

At The Brownstone Class—my acting studio in New York City—we train for something else. Our philosophy is different. We don't ask actors to relive trauma. We don't romanticize pain. We don't equate stillness with honesty. We teach actors to prepare not for the scene, but for the storm. To rehearse for disruption. To train their imagination. To use their body. To arrive not with a fixed performance, but with the ability to respond—honestly, freshly, and fully—to what's actually happening.

What if real doesn't mean small?
What if emotional truth isn't found in memory, but in action? What if naturalism is not the peak of acting—but a mask we're long overdue to rip off?

Before we go further, let me say this plainly:

I am not a household name.

I'm not a series regular. I haven't won an Emmy. You won't find a string of blockbusters on my IMDb page.

And yet, I've devoted my life to acting.

I've stood in audition rooms with my heart pounding and no rehearsal. I've hit marks on freezing pavement in the middle of the night. I've taped scenes alone in tiny apartments, hoping the work was enough to break through the noise. I've coached actors who booked—and didn't. I've taught classes to brilliant unknowns who deserved the same chance I've fought for.

I know this business can be brutal. I know what it means to give everything to a craft that doesn't always give back.

And that's why I teach.

It's not about having "made it." It's about making something that matters.

I've built a room where actors feel seen. Where we take the work seriously, not ourselves. Where we reclaim realism, imagination, and craft in an industry that increasingly mistakes imitation for truth.

I'm not writing this book to lecture from a pedestal. I'm writing it from the trenches.

I know what it feels like to question your path. To wonder if the world will ever catch up to what you know you can do. I've lived that doubt. I still live it. But I've also seen what happens when an actor stops waiting for permission and starts preparing for the truth. When they stop trying to "be real" and start making meaning.

That's what this book is about.

You don't have to be recognized by the world to do undeniable work.

You just have to be ready to hold the mirror—and decide where to aim it.

This book offers a prescription—
but not one carved in stone.
It's not a doctrine.
It's a revolt against dead training.
A call to reclaim what performance is for.

It's for every actor who has felt shackled by naturalism, isolated in preparation, or unseen by casting that asks for "real" without knowing what that means. It's for the teachers, too, the ones who wonder if there's more than sense memory or substitution. It's for the iconoclasts, the seekers, the storytellers who want to use their craft to disclose what's hidden beneath the noise.

At The Brownstone Class, we've tested these ideas in the studio, scene by scene, actor by actor. We've drawn from philosophy, psychology, classical training, and lived experience. We've re-read Stanislavsky, reinterpreted Chekhov, elevated Adler, and questioned Strasberg. We've combined theory and body, metaphor and precision, to forge a new path.

What follows is the foundation of that work. These chapters will trace the history of how we got here and propose a new way forward—one rooted in the belief that the actor is not a mirror, but the one who holds the mirror up to nature, and who decides where to aim it.

Because if we are to survive the age of illusion, we must stop trying to look real—and start making meaning.

If you're reading this, you're part of that revolution.

So walk with me. Let's dismantle some old myths. Let's reclaim realism. Let's reawaken imagination. Let's prepare for the truth behind the camera.

Let's begin.

Chapter One: Not a Day Like Any Other

"Treat it like it's just another day." But it isn't. Because if it were, it wouldn't be worth filming.

Ordinary days don't make good scenes. And good scenes don't stay ordinary for long. They start familiar. Quiet. Two people at breakfast. A voicemail. A hallway. But then—something shifts. A word lands wrong. A silence deepens. What was ordinary becomes irreversible.

Acting studios love to say: "Just be present. Just be truthful. Just be still."

But when has stillness ever changed a life? The camera doesn't roll for stillness—it rolls for transformation. And transformation doesn't begin in stillness. It begins in rupture. Something is risked. Something is revealed. Something breaks.

So no, it is not a day like any other. Not if we're doing our job. Not if the scene matters. Not if we're telling the truth.

Let's start off by being honest about this craft.

Screen Acting Is a Different Beast

Let's name what many teachers won't: screen acting is not stage acting with a smaller voice. It is a fundamentally different process.

In theatre, the actor is supported. They rehearse in ensemble, guided by a director. The world of the play is built around them over time—costumes, props, lights, sound, set. Each element gives them new information. The performance emerges gradually and communally.

But on camera? You get the script late. You might meet your scene partner minutes before filming. You may get one rehearsal—or none. The set might be a green screen. The lines might change mid-take. The direction you receive could be vague, contradictory, or missing entirely.

In theatre, 90% of the actor's preparation is done with others. In screen acting, 99% is done alone.

So how do you prepare? You prepare to be changed. You prepare to throw away your preparation. You prepare to see a new version of the scene on the day—and respond with truth. You prepare for anything.

What They Called Truth Wasn't the Whole Truth

You'll hear it all the time: "Truth is truth."

It sounds noble. Grounding. Egalitarian. But it's a dangerous half-truth.

Yes, truthful behavior is the goal. But truth must travel. It must be shaped. On stage, the truth must carry to the back of the house. It must ride breath, gesture, tempo. On screen, the truth must be real enough to hold up under magnification—unforced, unpolished, and undeniable in close-up.

Hamlet says it best:

"O'erstep not the modesty of nature."

The camera punishes even slight exaggeration. A single blink can say more than a monologue. The same truth that sings on stage can shriek on film.

To say "acting is acting" is to mistake intention for technique, and emotion for effectiveness. It's like saying swimming in a pool is no different than swimming in open ocean at night. Same motions. Entirely different realities.

Why We Get Frustrated

What frustrates us is not that teachers want to help—but that so many of them repeat certain phrases without recognizing their consequences. When someone says, "truth is truth" or "acting is acting," it's usually meant to simplify or encourage. But when those phrases are taken as doctrine, they become misleading.

Many actors spend years training for the theater and walk onto a film set completely unequipped. They're told to be smaller, quieter, stiller—without being told how. When their work doesn't land, they assume it's their fault.

Often, it isn't. It's the fault of an education that didn't take the medium seriously.

We're not angry at those who try to help. We're frustrated by the casualness—the way ideas are passed down like inherited furniture, never examined, just assumed to belong.

Most teachers don't realize the harm. They believe acting can be polished, but not taught. They believe talent is fixed. Innate. Mysterious.

But belief is not pedagogy.

And if you tell someone "just be truthful" without telling them what truth looks like at ten feet away through a 50mm lens, you haven't taught them. You've left them on their own.

I Was One of the Talented Ones

Now I'll admit: For me, the difference didn't feel huge. I'm one of those people for whom the process just worked. Like a musician with perfect pitch, I have a native sensitivity to drama—timing, tension, behavior. I can feel a scene snap into place. I can imagine fully.

That's not a boast. It's a confession. Because for a long time, I didn't really believe acting could be taught. Refined? Sure. Polished? Maybe. But not taught. Not from zero.

Most teachers don't believe it either. They assume a student must arrive with some intangible "it" factor. That all they can do is shape it, if it's there.

But that's not teaching. That's sorting.

This book is for those who weren't born gifted—and those who were, but were never taught how to train it. It teaches a way of thinking.

You won't rehearse toward control. You'll rehearse toward resilience. You won't aim to look truthful. You'll train to be changed by the moment. You won't memorize. You'll embody.

Not because truth isn't important. But because truth, without form, is nothing.

Truth must live in the vessel that can carry it. And the camera is a different vessel.

Spiritual Buoyancy

Stanislavsky insisted that actors develop "spiritual buoyancy"—the ability to float when everything shifts.

This isn't poetic.
It's technical.

You build buoyancy by training a process of variation, not a single performance.

Each preparation session is a laboratory:
change one variable, observe, adjust.

This elasticity is the actor's life jacket when everything goes sideways.

On set, pressure is the norm.
Time is short.
Lighting setups change.
Technical errors happen.

If your work relies on controlling the moment, you'll collapse when the moment doesn't cooperate.

But if your work trains you to stay responsive, the scene lives no matter what.

Seven Questions

We begin somewhere familiar.
Not to stay there—
but to recognize how far we still have to go.

Before we leave the cave entirely in Chapter Two, let's start here—with the kinds of questions every actor has heard, and few have truly explored:

Stanislavsky's Seven Character Questions are often taught as a checklist.

But in truth, they're an engine for variation, adaptation, and emotional range.

Don't treat them as something to answer once.
Use them as reps—repeatedly, flexibly—to prepare for change.

Each question, explored through multiple possibilities, becomes a tool for building responsiveness.

Here are the classic Seven Questions:

1. Who am I?
2. Where am I?
3. What time is it?
4. What do I want?
5. Why do I want it?
6. What will I do to get it?
7. What stands in my way?

They are usually taught in that order.
But in our work, that order is not sacred.

Sometimes you don't meet a character by asking who they are.
Sometimes you meet them by asking what they want—and realizing that want will change who they are.
Sometimes you meet them through where they are—and in finding the place, you uncover a different pressure on their time, their needs, their life.

A prison demands a different urgency than a hospital.
A hospital shapes different wants than a cemetery.

Place isn't just background.
It's a force that bends time, stakes, and behavior.

These questions are not fixed points.
They are variables.

And when you shift one, you shift the others.

By exploring these variables outside the given circumstances of the script, you free yourself from being trapped by what is merely stated.

You begin to discover the deeper needs, contradictions, and emotional currents that might have remained hidden if you only stayed within the narrow frame of the denoted story.

The text gives you what is visible.
The work of preparation reveals what is underneath.

And it is in that unseen, imaginative territory that the richest performances are born.

This is how you build a character capable of evolving under pressure—
not just repeating a plan.

Rethinking the Seven Questions

Let's break them down—and reframe how to approach them:

What do I want?

This is often taught as the scene objective.
But it's also a character question.

What you want might exist outside the immediate circumstances.

A character might want love, power, forgiveness, safety, revenge—long before the scene begins.

And that deeper want colors every objective in the scene.

For example, the character might want to win an argument (scene objective).
But underneath, what they really want is to be seen as competent by a parent who never believed in them.

The deeper want exists outside the scene's surface—
and yet it informs every tactic, every emotional beat.

Why do I want it?

This is the emotional engine.

But it's not just "why do I want this immediate goal?"—
it's why do I want what I want in life?

Is it fear of abandonment?
Hunger for validation?
Need for revenge?

The deeper your understanding of the why, the more naturally the emotional life of the scene will emerge.

The Other Questions — Reframed Dynamically

Who am I?
Name, profession, background, yes—but also shaped by what you want.

Where am I?
Environment affects want.
Unsafe spaces mutate needs.
Safe spaces reveal hidden ones.

What time is it?
Time is a pressure system.
Urgency arises from time.

What will I do to get it?
Tactics driven by need, not convenience.

What stands in my way?
Obstacles test the depth of want.

Building Variable Characters

In practice, you might not start with "Who am I?"
You might start with "What do I want?"
Or with "Where am I?"
Or with "What time is it?"

Each choice reverberates through the others.

Changing the answer to one variable creates a new character blueprint.

This is how you prepare for the real work—the collisions, the surprises, the director's shifting vision, the partner's new energy.

Preparation isn't about control.
It's about elasticity.
You're not building a perfect plan—
you're growing something that breathes.

In Chapter Ten, we'll return to these same questions—not as ideas, but as drills. Not as theory, but as conditioning. For now, we begin with them to reveal the depth this work demands

---

Exercises:

Exercise 1: The Calm Room Lies
Objective: Do nothing to show it. Let it leak through behavior, gaze, tempo, breath.

A silent scene—no dialogue. A doctor's office. A bench. A hallway.

Each actor enters the space carrying a hidden circumstance: grief, guilt, joy, terror. The audience doesn't know what it is—but the actor does.

Debrief:

What cracked the calm? What lived beneath the silence? What tension made it watchable?

Exercise 2: Prepare for Anything Reps

Choose a simple two-person scene.

Each actor prepares three distinct versions by answering the Seven Questions differently.

- One shallow (to win an argument)

- One relational (to gain forgiveness)

- One existential (to be saved)

Then rehearse each version. Let your partner's new behavior change you.

Debrief:

Which version surprised you? Which felt most alive? Which version felt most dangerous to play? This is where we begin. Not with certainty, but with possibility. Not with stillness. But with the wind.

Chapter Two: Out of The Cave

In the last chapter, we explored how the surface of a scene—the given circumstances—only shows part of the character's truth.

Now we turn to a deeper question:
What if everything we first perceive is only a shadow?

Let's begin in darkness.

In Book VII of *The Republic*, Plato offers one of the most enduring images in the history of thought—the Allegory of the Cave.

It's not just philosophy.
It's myth, metaphor, warning.
And it's also, in its way, an acting lesson.

A group of prisoners, chained since birth, sit facing a wall.
Behind them, a fire burns.
Between the fire and the prisoners, puppeteers pass objects along a walkway.
Their shapes—shields, animals, everyday items—cast shadows on the wall.

That's all the prisoners can see.
They can't turn their heads.
They've never seen the fire.
Never seen the people.

To them, the shadows are not reflections.
They are reality.

Now imagine one prisoner is released.
At first, he's disoriented.
Then he turns.
He sees the fire.
He stumbles outside.
The sun blinds him.
But slowly, his eyes adjust.
He sees the objects themselves.
The real things—trees, people, light.

And when he returns to the cave to tell the others, they laugh.
They don't believe him.
They cling to their shadows.

It's more than a parable.
It's the actor's dilemma.

The Script as Shadow

The script—the text, the structure, the lines—is the wall.
The shadow.
A flicker of something deeper.

The writer is the fire.
The lived experience, the emotional chaos, the heartbreak or revelation that cast the shadow in the first place.

And you, the actor, are the one being asked to turn.

Too many actors stay facing the wall.
They highlight the script.
Memorize beats.
Study intentions.

They take what's written as the full truth.

But the script is never the whole thing.
It's an echo.
It's residue.

Language is always a compromise—compressed, trimmed, stylized.

The real world that gave birth to the words is more complex than what appears on the page.

The truthful actor asks:

1.   What cast this shadow?

2. What pain shaped this monologue?

3. What fear shaped this silence?

4. What longing shaped this repetition?

Every line is a clue.
Every beat is a trace.

You don't just interpret dialogue—
you trace its source.
You don't just perform a character—
you investigate a world.

To do that, you must turn.

Realism vs. Naturalism

Too much modern training treats the script as the destination.
But the script is the trailhead.

Your job is to walk the path.
To ask harder questions.
To travel back to what the writer couldn't say—or didn't know they were saying.

This is realism—not naturalism.

Realism doesn't settle for the surface.
It searches for what lies beneath it.

It doesn't copy life as it appears.
It reveals life as it is felt.

1. Naturalism plays behavior.

2. Realism interrogates it.

3. Naturalism lives in the cave.

4. Realism climbs out.

5. Naturalism says, "This is how people talk."

6. Realism asks, "What is it costing them to say this?"

Realism is not documentary.
It is dramatized revelation.

Holding the Mirror

Shakespeare understood this.

In *Hamlet*, when the prince gives advice to the players, he doesn't say, "Become the mirror."
He says, "Hold the mirror up to nature."

That's an act.
A choice.
A framing.

The actor doesn't disappear.
The actor decides what the audience sees.

You are not the mirror's surface—
you are the hand that aims it.

And you must aim it well.

When Hamlet tells the actors to show "virtue her own feature, scorn her own image," he's not asking for mimicry.
He's asking for confrontation.
For truth.

The kind that makes the audience shift in their seats.

The kind that feels dangerous because it's real—
not because it's raw,
but because it's earned.

And that's the screen actor's responsibility:
To take a flat line and charge it with what it costs to say it.
To understand the unsaid.
To bring back what you saw when you left the cave.

When a character says, "I'm fine," and you know they aren't—
you don't play the lie.
You live in the truth beneath it.

That's realism.

Not volume.
Not effort.

But revelation.

The Script as Artifact

The script is not sacred.
It's a signal flare.

A record of the writer's attempt to capture something fleeting.

Every scene, every pause, every contradiction—
these are artifacts of an emotional or philosophical event that once lived inside someone.

When you hold a script, you're holding evidence.
A trace of a lived internal world.

Don't just study it.
Investigate it.

Don't just memorize it.
Question it.

Because behind that well-written scene is a human truth that couldn't be fully written down.

And your job—the sacred part of this craft—
is to make that truth live again.

The Return from the Fire

When you turn from the wall—
when you walk out of the cave and find the fire, the trees, the light—
it changes you.

You can't unsee it.
You can't pretend the script is all there is.

And when you bring that back into your work, something happens.

The performance deepens.
The lines stretch wider.
The silences start to mean more.

The scene breathes.

You are no longer playing the text.
You are playing what shaped it.

That's the kind of work that reaches people.
That lingers.

That doesn't just look like life—
it feels like recognition.

Because you've brought back the fire.

The script gives us what is visible.
The actor's work is to discover what isn't.

So go find it.

Exercises:

Exercise 1: Shadow and Source
Objective: Uncover the deeper emotional source behind scripted behavior.

1. Choose a short, dialogue-heavy scene.

2. Read it aloud once without commentary.

3. Ask: What is each line a shadow of? What emotion, memory, or truth might have generated that line?

4. Assign actors to speak the 'shadow' (the line as written), then immediately name the 'source' (the unspoken truth that cast it).

Debrief:

Which lines felt deeper when their source was exposed? How did this shift performance or awareness?

Exercise 2: Back to the Fire
Objective: Push actors beyond naturalism by asking philosophical questions of the text.

1. Select a scene with subtle or mundane conflict.

2. Actors answer: What larger human experience is this moment a metaphor for?

3. Have them play the scene again—not 'bigger,' but with this idea actively living under the behavior.

Debrief:

How did meaning change? What surprised the actor about the truth beneath the lines?

Chapter Three: The Meaning of Realism

Realism has been misunderstood—not just by audiences, but by actors, teachers, and directors alike.

Especially in American actor training, realism is often confused with naturalism.
And the consequences of that confusion run deep.

When we speak of "realism" here, we are speaking about a tradition—**American Realism**—born in the plays of Eugene O'Neill, Arthur Miller, Tennessee Williams, Clifford Odets, and others.

It is a theatrical style, shaped by specific cultural conditions, and it became the foundation for much of American film and television performance.

But its meaning has been distorted over time.

In contemporary actor training, particularly for the camera, realism is often treated as naturalism.

The two are not the same.

At a glance, they can look similar—restrained performances, muted emotions, everyday behavior.
But the resemblance is only surface deep.

While they may share techniques or tonal choices, their philosophical underpinnings diverge entirely.

Naturalism seeks to mimic life as it appears.
It prioritizes behavioral accuracy—the rhythms of daily interaction, the unremarkable details of ordinary life.

The actor often aims to disappear into the role, to perform believability so thoroughly that they seem to vanish.

But realism—true American Realism—is not about vanishing.

Realism is about making meaning.

Realism doesn't merely replicate what life looks like.
It reveals what life means.

It does not aim for invisible performance, but for essential performance—one that shows us what we have missed, what lies beneath the visible.

Realism, at its best, does not settle for what the eye can see.
It reaches for what the eye alone cannot name—the underlying forces, contradictions, and needs that shape human life from underneath the surface.

Where naturalism asks the actor to imitate behavior, realism asks the actor to interrogate behavior.

This is not an aesthetic distinction.
It's a spiritual one.

Because the truth is, life as it appears is often dull.
Repetitive.
Disconnected.

And unless we illuminate what lies beneath that surface, there's no reason to watch it unfold.

The Ubiquity—and Danger—of Naturalism

Let's be honest: naturalism is everywhere.

We see it in the shuffle of feet, the mumbling of lines, the casual glances.
It has become so pervasive in modern screen work that it's nearly invisible.

And that's the danger.

When we confuse the trappings of realism—its restraint, its subtlety—for realism itself, we lose the point.

Realism is not a tone.
It is a contract.

You, the actor, agree to make meaning out of the mundane.
You agree to hold something in the silence.
You agree to raise the stakes, to ask better questions, to pursue deeper motives.
You agree to reveal—not replicate.

Behavior Without Stakes Is Just Behavior

Imagine two people in a café.

In one version, they behave exactly as they would in real life—sipping coffee, checking their phones, exchanging polite banter.

It looks real.
But nothing is at stake.
Nothing changes.

That's naturalism.

Now imagine the same café.
But one character is hiding something: a betrayal, a terminal diagnosis, a plan to leave.

The behavior may still appear subtle—but now, there is tension.
Urgency.
Consequence.

That's realism.

Realism is not about doing more.
It's about exposing more.

The power doesn't come from volume—
it comes from depth.

Naturalism rests in the behavior.
Realism asks:

1. What motivates this behavior?

2. What threatens it?

3. What does it cost to maintain?

This is why realism is inseparable from stakes.

Because if nothing is at stake, nothing is happening.

And if nothing is happening, there's nothing worth watching.

What Realism Actually Demands

Let's clarify what realism demands of the actor:

1. It demands that you make behavior meaningful—not just accurate.

2. It demands that you locate the tension inside the stillness.

3. It demands that you make what's unsaid more compelling than what's spoken.

Great screen actors understand this instinctively.

Think of Mahershala Ali's performance in *Moonlight*, or Frances McDormand in *Nomadland*.

These are not performances that vanish.

They shape what we see.

The actors are not behaving; they are bearing witness to something profound—
and their presence is charged with intention.

Ali doesn't need to announce wisdom.
It lives in the space between his silences.

McDormand doesn't emote broadly.
But her choices frame every landscape, every glance, every goodbye.

That's realism.

From Reflection to Point of View

Realism is not about the actor disappearing.

It's about the actor standing in the scene as a point of view.

Not to blend in, but to show us something we wouldn't otherwise see.

To illuminate the inner pressure beneath an everyday moment.
To reveal the gravity under the ordinary.
To turn behavior into meaning.

That's your job.

Realism is not subtle mimicry.
It's precise revelation.

It is a performance with intention, with emotional stakes, with pointed observation of what it means to be human—especially when no one's looking.

Let naturalism give you texture.
Let realism give you purpose.

And then, do the work to make that purpose visible on screen.

Because realism, once reclaimed, can become something even larger than a style—
it can become a way of seeing.

Exercises:

Exercise 1: Same Scene, Two Realities
Objective: Help actors distinguish between naturalism and realism in performance.

1. Choose a short two-person scene with emotional undercurrents.

2. Perform it first as 'naturalistically' as possible. Keep it casual. Focus on behavior.

3. Then, ask actors to re-approach the scene, identifying what is at risk for each character. What are they hiding? What could they lose? Perform it again, this time with consequence.

Debrief:

Which version felt more alive? What shifted when stakes were acknowledged? What did the audience feel differently?

Exercise 2: The Risk Beneath the Line
Objective: Train actors to identify and activate subtext and hidden stakes.

1. Give each actor a neutral line (e.g., 'I'm fine,' 'You look tired,' 'We should go.').

2. Assign a secret that contradicts the line (e.g., they are heartbroken, terrified, hiding something).

3. Perform the line truthfully but with the internal reality shaping delivery.

Debrief:

How did contradiction impact expression? What does realism look like when words lie and the body tells the truth?

Chapter Four: The Group Theatre's Beautiful Mistake

The Group Theatre changed American acting.

They brought working-class stories to the stage.
They rejected melodrama.
They believed in emotional honesty.

They broke from the polished, presentational styles of their predecessors and leaned into the messy, domestic rhythms of American life.

They made the kitchen sink sacred.

But somewhere along the way, they lost the thread.

They mistook naturalism for depth.
They mistook stillness for truth.
They replaced stakes with subtlety.

And over time, their revolution flattened into routine.

Let's be clear—they meant well. And they left behind some indispensable tools.

But their legacy, when adopted uncritically, has limited generations of actors.

What They Got Right

The Group Theatre was founded in 1931 by Harold Clurman, Cheryl Crawford, and Lee Strasberg.

It was conceived as an American ensemble company inspired by Konstantin Stanislavsky's Moscow Art Theatre.

Their mission: to bring socially relevant, psychologically rich drama to the American stage.

They responded to the theatrical bloat of their time with something radical:
realism rooted in ordinary life.

They staged plays where the furniture creaked and the sinks ran.
Their sets looked like real apartments.
Their actors wore street clothes.

They turned domestic life into drama.

For audiences used to bombast and pageantry, this felt new.
It felt honest.
Democratic.
Revolutionary.

And for a time, it was.

But as often happens with revolutions, the aesthetic overtook the mission.

The Illusion of Realism

The Group's work appeared more truthful than it was because the sets looked familiar.

Audiences saw furniture they recognized, accents they heard at home—and they confused that recognition with revelation.

But great acting doesn't come from a faucet that works.
It comes from what happens when the water is shut off—and no one knows why.

Their realism was rooted in surface—the appearance of truth.

And it worked, until it didn't.

Over time, the aesthetic of authenticity began to replace the pursuit of meaning.

When naturalism becomes the ceiling, not the floor, the story begins to suffocate.

From Emotion to Behavior

The Group became fixated on behavior.
Subtle shifts.
Naturalistic rhythms.
They avoided theatricality.

But in doing so, they often avoided drama.

Emotion was replaced by implication.
Character was replaced by pattern.
Drama was replaced by mood.

This was most evident in their approach to performance: Stanislavsky's emphasis on given circumstances and psychological action gave way to a narrow focus on realism-as-behavior.

Actors began to believe that a scene should resemble life as it is lived—not life as it is felt.

And for a while, audiences leaned in.
But eventually, they leaned back.
They got bored.

What had been mistaken for realism was often just quietness.

And quietness, on its own, does not make meaning.

The Political Influence

It's important to understand the political context.

Many of the Group's members were socialists.
Their mission was not only artistic, but ideological.

They wanted to reflect the working-class experience.

They believed in exposing economic hardship, systemic injustice, and everyday struggle.

But their materialist worldview bled into their art.

Imagination—once the actor's greatest ally—became suspect.

It wasn't practical.
It wasn't political.
It wasn't "real."

Their plays were grounded in labor, routine, and emotional suppression.

The world outside the apartment set was too often ignored.

The myth of the "authentic working-class moment" began to supersede transformation.

The result: a kind of dramatic minimalism where stakes were implied but never escalated, and where stillness was mistaken for truth.

The Danger of Material Naturalism

The Group's aesthetic trained actors to believe that truth lives in behavior.

But truth lives in action.
In risk.
In contradiction.
In the stakes beneath the surface.

They traded transformation for transcription.

And slowly, the audience drifted.

Not all at once.
But over time.

They went to musicals.
To film.
To stories that still knew how to elevate life into something meaningful—without reducing it to its surface textures.

Adler Leaves the Cave

Stella Adler, one of the Group's most brilliant actors and a founding member, saw the danger early.

In 1934, she traveled to Paris to study directly with Stanislavsky.
But not the early Stanislavsky of affective memory—the one Strasberg and others had enshrined.

She studied with the elder master, the one who had moved on.

By then, he was exploring imagination, physical action, stylization.

He had collaborated with Vsevolod Meyerhold, the radical Russian director known for biomechanics.
He had seen Michael Chekhov—his most imaginative disciple—perform.

Adler returned with fire.

She declared that the Group had misunderstood their own idol.
That they had enshrined a ghost.

She warned them: memory was not enough.
Personal pain was not the path.
The actor must turn outward—to the world, to the text, to the body, to the imagination.

They ignored her.
She left.

The Beautiful Mistake

So yes, the Group Theatre mattered.

They broke new ground.
They changed the field.
They gave voice to a generation of actors.

They taught us to listen, to breathe, to sit in the silence between words.

But they also passed down a style that was small, cautious, and emotionally muted.

One that prized authenticity over transformation.
One that privileged personal history over shared imagination.

They made naturalism look like realism.

And in doing so, they passed down a limitation disguised as truth.

It's a beautiful mistake—but a mistake, nonetheless.

And if we are to reclaim the power of realism, we must evolve past it.

Exercises:

Exercise 1: The Set Doesn't Save You
Objective: Shift focus from environment to emotional truth.

1. Create a mock domestic scene with real props (table, phone, chair).

2. Have actors create a scene where the stakes are purely emotional—something must be confessed, hidden, or exposed.

3. Repeat the same scene with the props removed.

Debrief:

What changed? Did losing 'realism' in the set uncover something deeper in the performance?

Exercise 2: The Imagined World

Objective: Train the imagination independent of staging.

1. Assign a scene without any props or physical setting.

2. Actors must vividly imagine their environment—sounds, textures, smells.

3. Perform the scene again, responding fully to the imagined world.

Debrief:

What new behaviors or emotions emerged? How did the actor's imagination shape their choices?

Chapter Five: Strasberg and the Tyranny of the Inner Life

Lee Strasberg changed the game.

But he also changed the stakes—and not always for the better.

His method of emotional recall, born from his interpretation of Stanislavsky's early work, asked actors to reach inward. To mine memory. To source emotion from personal trauma.

And for many, this was a revelation.

But for too many others, it became a trap.

The Method taught actors that truth lived in the past.
That to cry on camera, you had to remember the moment your mother left.
That to rage, you had to conjure the bully who made you feel small.

It asked the actor to become their own wound.

It made suffering the measure of sincerity.

And while this led to some iconic performances—from Brando's vulnerability in On the Waterfront to De Niro's ferocity in Raging Bull—it also led to a culture of emotional exhibitionism.

A world where what was prized was not the clarity of the story, but the visibility of pain.
Where catharsis was mistaken for craft.

Feeling Isn't the Goal

Here's the heresy: feeling something isn't the same as acting truthfully.

You can cry in a scene and still fail to tell the story.

You can shake with rage and still make the audience feel nothing.

Because feeling, in itself, is not the point.

What matters is what the audience feels.

What matters is the action you pursue, the stakes you hold, the pressure you endure.

Emotion, if it arrives, is a byproduct of doing—not the objective.

Strasberg made feeling the finish line.

But feeling is not the scene.

The scene is a series of actions undertaken with purpose, shaped by conflict, and defined by change.

The Trap of Memory

Emotional recall trains the actor to loop back through their own life.
To substitute the character's world for their own.

But that loop can become a cage.

You become the scene's emotional supplier rather than its investigator.

And once you've trained to rely on yourself—your grief, your shame, your scars—you limit your range to the scope of your autobiography.

And while your life may be deep, it is not universal.

That's not art.
That's self-reference.

It can create a performance that is technically impressive and personally draining, but emotionally isolated.

The audience sees you feel, but they do not feel with you.

The connection does not cross the footlights—or the lens.

This is the tyranny of the inner life.

Stanislavsky Moved On

This is the great irony: Strasberg built his empire around a version of Stanislavsky that Stanislavsky himself had outgrown.

By the 1930s, Stanislavsky had moved away from affective memory.

He recognized its psychological toll and its limitations.

He had begun working with physical action, imagination, and what he called the "method of physical actions"—a system that emphasized objective-driven behavior, rooted in the body and shaped by circumstance.

He understood what Strasberg didn't:
That emotion follows behavior.
That the body is not a servant to the past, but a gateway to the present.

You don't need to cry about your own father to play King Lear.

You need to understand power, aging, and loss—and then pursue those truths through action.

Action is the pathway.
Emotion is the echo.

This wasn't theory for Stanislavsky—it was evolution.

He had seen the mental and physical strain of emotional memory.

He had watched actors collapse inward.

And he had the courage to change.

When It's All About You, the Story Suffers

An actor chasing their own feeling is not serving the scene.

They're trying to be seen.

And while vulnerability is sacred, performance is not therapy.

The actor's responsibility is not to feel—it is to make meaning.

The camera doesn't care what you're feeling if it doesn't serve the story.

And the audience can sense when they're watching an actor perform themselves.

You may be honest—but you're not revealing anything.

Not about the character.
Not about the human condition.
Not about the world.

You've simply invited us into your personal archive.

That's not performance.
That's exposure.

The Mirror Is a Weapon

Let's clarify this:

Acting is not the mirror.
The actor is not the mirror.

The mirror is the tool you hold.

Like Hamlet's directive—to *"hold, as 'twere, the mirror up to nature"*—the actor must aim the mirror.

Choose what it reflects.
Decide what the audience must see.

The mirror is not passive.
It is not neutral.

It is active.
It is weaponized.

It is the way we make our choice clear.
It is how we say, *"This is what matters in this moment. This is the truth beneath the scene."*

We wield the mirror.
We do not become it.

The actor's job is not to reflect life back as it appears.

It is to decide which part of life to make visible—and why.

And when that visibility is in service of story, the audience leans forward.

They're not moved by your suffering.
They're moved because you've shown them something they didn't know they knew.

We Must Reclaim the Work

The work is not about what's inside you.

The work is about what's happening between you and the world of the scene.

It is external, active, vivid.
It moves. It breathes. It reacts.

It is the mirror you carry into battle.

And when used with integrity, it displays something the audience can no longer ignore.

We don't reject vulnerability here.
We demand it be rooted in something real.

It's a redefinition of it.

Vulnerability isn't reliving your trauma.
It's surrendering to the moment—even when that moment is unfamiliar, uncomfortable, and imagined.

The Method gave actors a language for truth.

But it's time we gave them a language for freedom.

Exercises:

Exercise 1: Do It, Don't Feel It
Objective: Help actors understand that action generates emotion.

1. Assign a scene with a strong objective (e.g., to seduce, to warn, to win).

2. Actors must pursue this objective with total commitment—without prepping internal emotion.

3. No memory recall allowed. Only action.

Debrief:

What feelings emerged naturally? Did the lack of internal prep free or block the performance?

Exercise 2: Memory vs. Imagination

Objective: Contrast personal memory with imaginative circumstances.

1. Assign two actors the same emotional beat (e.g., grief or rage).

2. One uses emotional recall. The other builds a detailed imagined scenario.

3. Perform both and compare.

Debrief:

Which felt more vivid? Which was more sustainable? Which felt more rooted in the scene?

Chapter Six: What Stella Knew

Stella Adler broke from the Group Theatre not because she rejected realism, but because she saw the prison that naturalism had become.

While others were mining memory, she was cultivating imagination.

While others turned inward for truth, she turned outward—for life, for literature, for circumstance.

Adler knew something that has been all but forgotten in modern screen acting:

You don't become the material.
You carry it.
You shape it.
You let it speak.

You do not use your own trauma to animate the role.
You use the world.

Not because your life lacks value, but because your imagination has greater range.

What She Saw—and What She Left Behind

Adler studied with Stanislavsky at a critical juncture in his evolution.

He had moved beyond the affective memory of his early period—the very practice that had become gospel within the Group under Lee Strasberg.

Instead, Stanislavsky was experimenting with physical action, external stimuli, and imaginative construction.

He had grown weary of what memory-based acting did to performers: it isolated them, narrowed their emotional range, and often retraumatized them in pursuit of "truth."

Adler was paying attention.

And when she returned from Europe, she returned with a warning: The Group had enshrined a version of Stanislavsky that the man himself had long since left behind.

Acting Is Not Self-Exposure. It's Self-Transcendence.

For Adler, acting was not therapy. It was not confession.

It was not about reliving your father's death or your first heartbreak in front of a camera.

It was about enlarging the self to meet the world of the play.

She taught that to be an actor, you had to become a student of humanity.
Of history. Of architecture. Of politics. Of class systems. Of literature. Of faith. Of contradiction.

You could not play a 16th-century noble, a street preacher in 1930s Harlem, or a revolutionary in post-colonial India if your only tool was your own life.

This wasn't theory. It was survival.

The imagination, she argued, was not just a tool of artistry—it was the actor's only real freedom.

Imagination Over Memory

Memory is limited to what happened.

Imagination opens the door to what could happen.

Adler trained actors to build not a recollection, but a circumstance.

To craft the world in vivid detail:
The chipped edge of a prison wall.
The sound of a train that never comes.
The tremble of a letter in your hand before it's read.

This is not pretending.

This is preparation.

And it is far more sustainable than substitution.

Memory may dry up.
But the imagination, when disciplined and specific, becomes infinite.

The Body Responds to Imagination

This is where Adler's lineage intersects with Michael Chekhov, Stanislavsky's most spiritually expansive disciple.

Chekhov taught that the body could not help but react when immersed in strong imaginative work.

That the muscles, breath, and voice would align with a vividly imagined world—without the actor needing to dig into personal grief.

Adler agreed.

And in her teachings, the actor's job was not to feel—but to build.

When the circumstances were alive, when the stakes were clear, when the world was richly imagined, the body responded.

Truth appeared.
Not because the actor forced it.
But because they had earned it.

This Is Realism

It's important to say this clearly: Adler was not rejecting realism. She was reclaiming it.

Realism is not naturalism.

It is not the illusion of daily life.

It is the pursuit of meaning through the imagined life.

It is specificity, urgency, consequence—qualities that can only be generated when the actor uses their full range of creative faculties.

Imagination is not a departure from realism.
It is its deepest source.

The Actor Is a Citizen of the World

Adler believed actors had a civic duty—not just to entertain, but to witness.

To speak for the unseen.
To give shape to the interior life of others.

She demanded that her students read voraciously, travel widely, and study the cultures, beliefs, and systems outside their own experience.

Because when the character comes from another century, another faith, another gender—you will not find them in your diary.

You will find them in your curiosity.

What looks like elitism from the outside
is freedom from illusion on the inside.

It is the belief that the actor's reach should always exceed their grasp.

That performance is not about what you've survived—but what you're willing to build.

Her Legacy—Our Future

Adler left us a model of performance that did not collapse under emotional recall.

She gave us a pedagogy rooted not in excavation, but in expansion.

She taught us to aim the mirror not at ourselves, but at the world—and to decide what truth must be seen.

She reminded us that vulnerability does not require autobiography.

And that the greatest courage is not in revealing our own pain, but in telling someone else's truth with integrity.

We are not broken things made into art.

We are artists making sense of a broken world.

That is what Stella knew.

Exercises:

Exercise 1: The World of the Character
Objective: Use research and imagination to build external truth.

1. Assign each actor a character from a different historical period or social class.

2. Ask them to construct the character's world—clothing, setting, voice, values—through research.

3. Perform a neutral scene from that character's imagined world.

Debrief:

How did building the outer life affect inner stakes and behavior? What did research unlock that memory could not?

Exercise 2: Five Senses of the Scene
Objective: Strengthen the actor's imaginative sensory recall.

1. Assign a setting (e.g., a rooftop at night, a courtroom, a childhood home).

2. Ask actors to vividly describe the scene using all five senses.

3. Perform a scene in that imagined environment.

Debrief:

What sensations influenced performance? Which details grounded emotional

Chapter Seven: Realism Reclaimed — Hamlet Was a Director

Before Stanislavsky.
Before Strasberg.
Before Adler.
Before the Group Theatre.
Before the Method.
Before cinema—
there was Hamlet.

And Hamlet—arguably the greatest fictional actor and director in literature—
had a clear philosophy about the craft.

His instructions to the players in Act III, Scene II of *Hamlet* are not vague poetic musings.
They are a compact acting manifesto.
A vision of realism that still outpaces many modern pedagogies.

Earlier, we distinguished realism from naturalism—
clarifying that realism is not surface imitation,
but the revelation of deeper meaning.

Now, we turn to reclaim realism fully:
Not just as a style, but as a way of seeing, choosing, and creating for the screen.

Hold, as 'twere, the Mirror Up to Nature

This line has been so widely quoted it's lost its teeth.

But Hamlet does not say, "become the mirror."
He says, "hold" it.

To hold something is to exercise judgment.
Responsibility.
Authorship.

It implies direction.

To hold the mirror is not to vanish—
it is to frame.

And framing is power.

It determines what becomes visible—
and what remains unseen.

It determines what the audience is allowed to confront,
and what remains safely hidden.

The mirror, in Hamlet's hands, is not passive.
It is strategic.

Reflective, yes—
but also selective.

It is the actor's tool,
not the actor's identity.

This distinction is everything.

To Show Virtue Her Own Feature, Scorn Her Own Image

Hamlet is not advocating subtle mimicry.
He wants the players to wield performance as revelation—
to expose corruption, vanity, hypocrisy in the court.

He wants truth onstage to reveal lies offstage.

This is not decorative art.
It is ethical art.
It is art with consequence.

It's performance that wakes the sleeper,
that confronts illusion,
that turns the audience from spectators into witnesses.

This is what realism must do:
Not blend in—
but break through.

O, There Be Players That I Have Seen Play…

Hamlet's warning to the players is not about volume.
It is about falseness.

His critique is not of magnitude,
but of intention.

He criticizes actors who "out-Herod Herod"—
who perform so violently or artificially that they break the spell of truth.

But note: he is not arguing for smallness.
He is arguing for **clarity**.
For truth in proportion.
For performance as precision,
not performance as performance.

This is a vital corrective to modern misunderstandings of realism.

Realism isn't small.
It isn't casual.
And it sure as hell isn't muttering.

It is **truth that fits the moment.**

And sometimes that truth is large.
Sometimes it is still.
But it is never hollow.

What Hamlet Understood

Hamlet understood something many actor training programs have forgotten:
That realism is not about imitation—
but illumination.

He knew that honesty doesn't always arrive in whispers.
That stakes don't always come cloaked in subtlety.
That sometimes the only way to speak the truth
is to shout it—
or to say nothing at all and let the body carry the burden.

He knew that every line, every pause, every movement
must be in service of what matters *now*.

Because Hamlet is not merely putting on a play.
He is staging a confrontation.

His realism is strategic.
It is built to reveal.

This is the actor's task:
Not to blend in,
but to bring forth.

To aim the mirror where it hurts—
and where it heals.

Shakespeare Was a Realist

Modern actors are often taught that Shakespeare is "heightened," "stylized," or "classical."

But Shakespeare was writing **realism**.

His characters struggle with identity, power, betrayal, shame, love, death.

His plays ask hard questions and give no easy answers.

His language isn't ornamental.
It's precise.

It distills thought to its most essential form.

To play Shakespeare well is not to play "big."
It's to play **clearly.**

With need.
With structure.
With stakes.

It is not to perform poetry.
It is to reveal people.

Real ones.
Complex.
Contradictory.
Breathing.

Brecht's Hammer — A Proper Response to the Mirror

"Art is not a mirror held up to reality,
but a hammer with which to shape it."
— Bertolt Brecht

We are not the first to challenge the shallow reading of Hamlet's line.

Brecht saw through the same misunderstanding.

He didn't attack Shakespeare—
he attacked the way later generations reduced "the mirror" to passive mimicry.

In the hands of 20th-century realism,
the mirror became literal:

**Vanish into the role. Disappear into the behavior.
Let the audience forget you're even performing.**

But Hamlet never said "become the mirror."
He said **hold** it.

And Brecht understood what that meant.

Brecht refused the notion that acting was merely reflection.
He demanded that it be construction.
Intervention.

A deliberate act of framing.

Not naturalism—
but truth by distortion.

Not behavior—
but belief interrogated.

He was not a realist.
And that's important.

He didn't want the audience to forget they were watching a play—
he wanted them to remember.

He used contradiction.
Commentary.
Direct address.

He broke the illusion to expose the system.
He interrupted comfort to restore clarity.

He knew what Hamlet knew:

**That the actor must not just reflect the world.
They must shape how we see it.**

And sometimes, the mirror must be broken.

Because realism without purpose is camouflage.
But realism with aim?

That's a weapon.

Hamlet's Legacy for the Modern Actor

You are not here to behave.
You are here to expose.

To reflect.
To frame the world with your performance.

You are not the mirror.
You decide what it reflects.
You decide where it points.
You decide what truth must be seen.

Realism is not submission.
It is intention.

It is the actor saying:
"This matters. Right now. Look."

And he does this by living the stakes,
not by construction.

That's what Hamlet knew.

And that's what you must reclaim.

Not just to act—
but to change what the audience believes is possible.

To hold the mirror is the actor's task.
But learning how to see what the mirror reveals—
that is the next discipline.

Exercises:

Exercise 1: Angle the Mirror
Objective: Train actors to interpret and frame rather than behave.

1. Choose a short Shakespearean or heightened monologue.

2. Ask the actor to prepare three interpretations:

- One reflecting virtue.

- One reflecting scorn.

- One reflecting the present cultural moment.

3. Perform each and reflect on the shift in meaning.

Debrief:

How did intention reshape the scene? What angle felt most urgent?

Exercise 2: Empty vs. Earned
Objective: Distinguish between theatricality and truth.

1. Assign a speech with high emotion.

2. Perform it once 'big'—full Herod.

3. Then rebuild it with stakes and structure from within.

Debrief:

What changed? Which felt connected? Which was louder—and which was real?

Chapter Eight: The Art of Seeing

Imagination is not a luxury.
It is a tool for survival.

For the actor, it's the difference between reacting truthfully and pretending.
Between responding to real circumstances—or faking ones you barely believe in.

Yet modern training continues to treat imagination like a soft skill.
Something creative, yes—but peripheral.
Something for dreamers.
Not something central to technique.

That assumption is wrong.
And it's hurting actors.

Passive and Active Imagination

Let's make a crucial distinction.

Passive imagination is involuntary.
It's the anxiety spiral.
The worst-case scenario at 3 a.m.
The vision that creeps in when you're walking alone at night.
It's rich, intense, high-resolution.

Imagination isn't fantasy.
It's how we survive what's real.

Now contrast that with active imagination—the deliberate ability to conjure circumstances, sensations, or images at will.

Most actors have strong passive imagination and weak active imagination.
But that's backward.
Because in performance, the only imagination that matters is the one you can control.

And that control can be trained.

The Problem with Most Actor Prep

You're handed a script.
You run lines.
You find the beats.
You maybe get a costume.
You hope the set gives you something to respond to.

And if it doesn't?
You rely on what you know.
On your life.
Your history.
Your default behavior.

This is fine—until the story isn't about you.
Until the given circumstances ask you to live in a world you've never been in.

Now your memory betrays you.

Only imagination can save you.

Training Imagination Is Training Empathy

To imagine something with detail—to really build it in your mind—is to experience it viscerally.

The body doesn't always distinguish between imagined stimulus and real stimulus.

This is why athletes visualize success.
Why soldiers rehearse missions mentally.
Why therapists use guided imagery.

It's not about escape.
It's about precision.

Actors must do the same.

Build the World Before You Feel the Feeling

Don't try to cry.
Don't try to shake.
Don't try to "play" love or fear.

Instead: build the hospital room.
Build the letter that didn't come.
Build the sound of your partner walking away.

Don't chase emotion.
Chase clarity.

If the image is vivid, the feeling will come.
And if it doesn't, the behavior will still be real.

Imagination is not about performance.
It's about presence.

Preparing for Anything Means Rehearsing Possibility

You're not preparing one version of a scene.
You're building multiple imagined realities:

1. What if this happens in winter instead of summer?

2. What if your partner is late? Or crying? Or whispering?

3. What if the object is heavier than you thought?

Actors who do this can adapt.
On set.

On the fly.
Without panic.

Because they've rehearsed not the scene, but the stimulus.

Improvisation reacts.
Imagination leads.

Reclaiming the Muscle

Your imagination is already strong.
You've just been using it reactively.

Let's make it proactive.
Let's use it to create.
Let's train it with intention.
With stakes.
With discipline.

Because imagination isn't fluffy.
It's fierce.

It's your most powerful tool.
And it's time we treated it like one.

And like any tool, it must be sharpened.

Seeing fully is the first act of creation.
And creation is where the real work begins.

Exercises:

Exercise 1: The Object Doesn't Exist
Objective: Create believable imaginary objects.

Each actor chooses a personal object from their character's life (e.g., a letter, a gun, a necklace).

They must describe its sensory details: weight, temperature, smell, texture, age.

Interact with it silently, then speak a line from the scene.

Debrief:
How did vivid physical detail shape behavior and tone?
Could others believe the object was real?

Exercise 2: Before the Scene
Objective: Build emotional pre-life through sensory detail.

Before performing, actors spend two minutes vividly imagining what just happened.

Who were they with? What space were they in? What did they hear, feel, smell?

Enter the scene with that lived reality.

Debrief:
Did the imagined world affect presence?
Was the scene richer emotionally?

Chapter Nine: Preparation for Collision

Seeing is not passive.
Imagination is not passive.
And action must never be passive.

The actor doesn't prepare for a scene to recreate a performance.
They prepare to collide with it—to meet shifting stimulus with a living, breathing, embodied truth.

The mind imagines.
But it is the body that meets the world.

The Body as Muse

The modern actor is often taught to begin with feeling.
We ask ourselves, "What would I feel here?" or "How do I access this emotion?"—as if the answer lives in memory.

But what if it doesn't?
What if the most direct route to emotion isn't backward—but downward?
Into the body, not the brain.

The body doesn't lie.
It doesn't stall or justify.
It reacts.
It absorbs.
It reveals.

And in the actor's work, it becomes the muse.

Walk Before You Speak

Before the character speaks, they move.
And how they move tells us everything:

1. The anxious or intellectual character may lead with the head—jutting forward, searching for certainty.

2. The confident character leads with the chest—upright, forward, exposing the heart.

3. The sexual character leads with the hips—loose, grounded, responsive.

4. The checked-out or dull character may throw their feet forward with effort.

Not a sketch—
a scaffolding.
The body thinks before the words arrive.

Chekhov's Forgotten Genius

Michael Chekhov—Stanislavsky's most innovative disciple—knew that the body could unlock the emotional life faster than memory.

He gave us Psychological Gesture: a full-bodied, expressive movement that manifests character intention.
He gave us Archetypal Gesture: simplified, symbolic physical expressions of fundamental drives—reaching, grasping, pushing, protecting.

You don't play grief.
You bend under it.
You don't act love.
You reach for it.
You don't summon rage.
You thrust it forward.

And the emotion appears—not because you chased it, but because you invited it through form.

The Body Is an Emotional Trigger

This is biology.
The body responds to posture, tension, and gesture long before the brain processes it.

If you slump, you feel shame.
If you puff your chest, you feel pride.
If you cover your mouth, your breath shortens—and anxiety creeps in.

Change the shape, change the state.

This is not about style.
It's about stimulus.

Sensation Over Substitution

This is the pivot of the work:

Stop substituting your own life.
Start generating the character's life—through physical sensation.

When you walk in their shoes—literally, physically, musically—you begin to think their thoughts.
The body leads, and the mind follows.

Substitution shrinks the work.
Sensation expands it.

The Mind Will Follow the Body

This is not a metaphor—it's a practice.

If you shape the spine, you shape the story.
If you shift the breath, you shift the intention.

You don't need a backstory.
You need a backbone.

Too often, actors over-intellectualize their way into inaction.
They wait to "feel ready."

But readiness doesn't come from analysis.
It comes from rhythm, from weight, from kinetic truth.

This is how we reclaim realism—from the outside in.

Realism Is Not Shrinking—It's Honesty

To lead with the body is not to stylize.
It is to specify.
To uncover the truths that dialogue alone can't carry.

The audience may not name it—but they will feel it.
Because we are all tuned to bodies.
We read them.
Mirror them.
Respond to them.

And when the actor's body is living truthfully, nothing else needs to be explained.

This isn't mimicry.
It's shape with consequence.
It's form that births character—
not the other way around..

It is the body—not the memory—that opens the door to truth.

Collision is not chaos.
Collision is truth in motion.

Exercises:

Exercise 1: Walk the Psychology
Objective: Discover character through physical initiation.

Assign actors psychological states or character types: anxious, confident, desirous, defeated.

Ask them to walk across the room letting a different body part lead: head, chest, hips, feet.

Observe how the walk affects energy, breath, and mindset.

Debrief:
Which walk unlocked unexpected behavior?
Did a story or emotional state emerge from movement alone?

Exercise 2: Gesture into Emotion
Objective: Generate emotion through psychological gesture.

Have each actor choose a strong, full-body gesture that symbolizes a basic desire (e.g., to protect, to dominate, to connect).

Repeat the gesture fully, then let it fade while delivering a line from a scene.

Observe the residual physical impact.

Debrief:
What emotion surfaced?
Was the gesture more effective than emotional recall?

Chapter Ten: Prepare for Anything

A rehearsal is not a search for the perfect performance.
It is the building of resilience for when the perfect performance shatters.

In Chapter One, we exposed the lie of the calm room—the myth that preparation means stillness, safety, or control.
But naming the problem is not enough.
We have to build the solution.

This chapter is about constructing the kind of preparation that survives impact.
Not a performance to protect, but a body and imagination trained to meet the storm when it comes.

What does it mean to truly prepare for anything as a screen actor?
Not theoretically.
Not spiritually.
But practically, rigorously, artistically?

It means preparing in a way that liberates, not limits.
That adapts, not calcifies.
That builds a habit of transformation—not a performance to protect.

Build a Process, Not a Performance

Actors who treat preparation as a script-to-stage journey often forget the fundamental difference between theatre and screen.

In theatre, you have ensemble.
Rehearsals.
Weeks to build.

In screen work, you may get one take—and zero prep with your partner.
That means you must build the world before you enter it.
And be ready to let it go the second you arrive.

Your process must be porous.
Curious.
Repetitive.
Exploratory.

Stanislavsky's Questions—Turned into Workouts

Take Stanislavsky's seven classic questions—and turn them into workouts:

1. Who am I?

2. Where am I?

3. What time is it?

4. What do I want?

5. Why do I want it?

6. What will I do to get it?

7. What stands in my way?

Now vary the answers.
Try five different wants.
Try three different reasons why.
Try the scene in a hospital, in a garden, in a club.
Try it at night.
At dawn.
In 1920.
In the year 3000.

You're not rehearsing.
You're conditioning.

You're building imaginative stamina.
Physical flexibility.
Emotional range.

And you're doing it before anything is fixed.

Why Variability Prepares You Better Than Mastery

If you've only prepared one version of the truth, you'll panic when asked to change it.

But if you've prepared ten, you'll recognize the new version as just another variation.

Now, you're not improvising.
You're selecting.
Reacting.
Reframing.

Because you've trained to let the scene breathe—and meet it there.

Let the Scene Change You

This is the ultimate discipline of screen acting:

To arrive with everything—and be willing to lose it.
To bring a world—and let it be changed by a line, a prop, a moment, a partner.

Actors call this being "in the moment."
But what it really is, is responsive imagination.
And it's earned through repetition, not randomness.

You don't need to be fearless.
You need to be flexible.

You don't need a perfect version.
You need a process that survives collision.

This is what it means to prepare for anything.
Not perfection.
Resilience.

Exercises:

Exercise 1: Three Versions

Objective: Build agility and emotional variety.

1. Choose a 2-person scene.
2. Perform it three ways:
   1. Want is shallow (e.g., to impress).
   2. Want is relational (e.g., to be forgiven).
   3. Want is existential (e.g., to be seen or saved).
   1. Discuss how each version changed behavior and emotional depth.

Debrief:
Which stakes surprised you?
Did deeper wants generate richer moments?

Exercise 2: 'What If?' Rehearsals
Objective: Rehearse under shifting conditions.

   1. Run the scene three times, altering imaginary context:
1. It's your last conversation.
2. You just learned a devastating secret.
3. The power goes out during the scene.

1. Perform the same dialogue, responding honestly to new context.

Debrief:
Which changes unlocked new energy?
How did preparation meet the unexpected?

Chapter Eleven: Lines, Lines, Lines

Memorization is not preparation.
It is the residue of real preparation—or the residue of panic.

Actors are obsessed with lines.
They panic about them.
They fixate on them.
They cram them in like students before an exam.

"I just need to get off book," they say.
As if that's the destination.
But the lines aren't the work—
they're what remains once the work is real.
And most of the time, they're chasing the shadow, not the source.

They think they'll do the "real acting" once the lines are locked in.
But if you've memorized the lines in a panic, from a place of fear and pressure, then that panic gets baked into the performance.

You can't cram from anxiety and expect to show up grounded.
It doesn't match.
It doesn't transfer.

Calmness Is a Lie, But Preparation Isn't

We talked in an earlier chapter about how calmness is a lie—that no serious actor I know steps onto set or into an audition feeling truly calm.
Not the good ones, anyway.

They feel nervous.
They feel adrenaline.
Because what they're doing is high risk.
Someone is watching.
Someone is judging.
Someone might be recording.

And that pressure is real.

But the best actors don't fight the nerves.
They don't pretend it's not happening.
They don't try to erase their fear before the slate.
They just carry it.
They've learned to perform with it.

Because they didn't build their prep around false calm.
They built it with readiness.

That's where relaxation—Stanislavsky's word—actually matters.
Not in the moment before "action," but in the days and hours leading up to it.

Relaxation doesn't mean lazy.
It doesn't mean chill.
It means open.
Responsive.
Non-panicked.

And most actors never get there.

They don't prepare in a place of relaxation.
They scramble.
They memorize late.
They do rote repetition.
They try to stuff the lines in from a place of anxiety, as if repetition alone will save them.
And then, right before the camera rolls, they suddenly try to "relax."

It's too late for that.

Don't Memorize the Lines, Marinate in Them

I've watched this hundreds of times—especially with self-tapes.

Actors look at the page and immediately try to hold the lines in their head.
They're chasing the words.
They don't want to mess up.
They're afraid of looking unprepared.

But they haven't done the deeper work.
The investigation.
The slow burn.

Now, granted, I'm someone to whom lines come easily.
But not always.

And I don't really try to "memorize" them anymore.
I don't rehearse for recall.
I rehearse for revelation.

I explore.
I change the answers to the seven questions.
I shift the objective.
I try a new costume piece.
I play an archetypal gesture.
I whisper the lines, then shout them.
I let the scene breathe, walk away, come back.

And little by little, the scene starts revealing itself.
I see new beats.
New stakes.
I start understanding why the character speaks the way they do—
and when I get there, the words are no longer hard to remember.

They're the only ones that make sense.

Memorization forces.
Preparation reveals.
The lines don't stick because you repeat them—
they stick because they matter.

The Words Remember You

Now, when coaching actors—especially on self-tapes—I see the same mistake.

They haven't built a real relationship with the words.
They either cling to them, afraid to forget one, or they casually paraphrase to sound more "natural."

That second one drives me nuts.

Because when I ask, "Why did the character say that word instead of this one?"—they usually don't know.
They haven't asked.
They haven't done the forensic work of looking at the exact language.

They're too focused on the idea of the scene, not the composition of it.

But words carry fingerprints.

Let's say the line is "I'm fine."
Why not "I'm okay"?
Or "I'm surviving"?
Or "I'm not dead"?

Each version shifts the tone.
The implication.
The need behind it.

And when you start asking why a character chose those specific words, it unlocks the script.
Even if the writer didn't consciously know what they were doing, the subconscious left clues.

And if you follow them—if you build a real connection to the words—you don't need to memorize.
The words will come find you.

The Script Isn't a Test

I don't care if the lines are exact in a self-tape.
I care if they're alive.

Harold Guskin, author of How to Stop Acting, said the most important connection an actor makes is to their dialogue.
Not because you need to get it "right" like a multiple-choice test.
But because the dialogue is the map.

It's the clue trail.
It's the artifact of the character's desire.

What they say—and what they don't—is the most direct line to their psychology.

I once directed a play and noticed something in the scene—how two characters used language to avoid intimacy.
It was written into the pauses.
The backpedals.
The awkward phrasing.

I pointed it out in rehearsal.
The writer, who was watching, sat back stunned.
He hadn't realized he wrote that.

It was unconscious.
But it was true.

When you train your imagination, when you listen to what's underneath the text, you start to discover things the writer didn't even know they left behind.

And that's where performance becomes revelation.
Not recitation.

The Real Work of Lines

So let's put this plainly:

1. Don't cram your lines.

2. Don't work in panic.

3. Don't "relax" right before a take if you didn't prepare that way.

4. Don't memorize—explore.

5. Ask: "Why these words and not others?"

6. Let the lines come to you through the action, the stakes, the objective, the truth of the character.

The lines are only shadows.
Trace them carefully—and you'll find the fire that cast them.

Exercises:

Exercise 1: The "Why Not That?" Drill
Objective: Unlock the necessity behind specific word choice.

Take any short line of dialogue from a script—no more than 5–7 words.

1. Ask yourself:

    1. Why this phrase instead of something else?

    2. What are five other ways this character could have said it?

    3. What do those alternatives reveal?

2. Return to the original line. What makes it necessary? What is the emotional or psychological cost behind choosing these words?

Debrief:
Move from viewing the line as a neutral instruction to experiencing it as a deliberate, character-driven choice.
You're not just speaking—you're revealing something inevitable.

Exercise 2: The Scene Without Lines

Objective: Discover why the written words matter by living the scene first.

1. Put the script down. Don't look at it.

2. Play the scene using only behavior, stakes, and objective. Say anything that comes to mind, as long as it's motivated by the given circumstances.

3. Once complete, return to the script and read the actual lines aloud. Let them hit you fresh.

Debrief:
Which lines now feel more precise than what you improvised?
Where did the writer's phrasing surprise you?
What did the written version express that your improvised one couldn't?

.

Chapter Twelve: The Power of Why

Plato gave us the cave.
Socrates gave us the question.

If *Out of the Cave* taught us to stop mistaking shadows for truth,
then this chapter asks:
How do we uncover what casts them?

The answer isn't found in memory.
It's found in inquiry.

And the sharpest tool we have is this:
Why?

You're not just playing a role.
You're interrogating a consciousness.

Each line, each beat, each silence—
these aren't choices to memorize.

They're evidence.
Clues about pressure.
Contradiction.
Illusion.
Desire.

Clues about what a person believes—
and what they're willing to betray to keep believing it.

When you ask why, you're not decorating the character.
You're excavating them.

Why vs. The Magic If

Stanislavsky's *magic if* asks:
What if I were this person, in this circumstance?

It's a powerful gateway.
But it invites substitution.
It asks you to place *yourself* into the given world.

Asking *why*, on the other hand, does something more rigorous.
It investigates the world itself.

The *magic if* lets you imagine your way in.
Why demands that you understand what the character is fighting to protect.

Philosophy Is Rehearsal for Integrity

Socrates used *why* not to destroy belief—
but to test it. Strip it down. See if it could stand.

Actors must do the same.

These aren't performance questions.
They're ethical ones.

They touch motive.
Integrity.
Self-deception.
Shame.
Longing.

They transform the actor from imitator into investigator.

Not someone who "plays a role"—
but someone who uncovers what a person is willing to lose to remain themselves.

The Line Is a Thesis

Every line of dialogue is a thesis the character is testing.

"I'm fine"
= I'm hoping this lie is enough to keep you out of my pain.

"You should go"
= I want you to stay, but I can't afford to need you.

"Nothing's wrong"
= Everything is wrong, but I have no name for it yet.

Each line reveals a theory about the world:
What the character thinks will work.
What they believe people want.
How they understand safety, power, connection.

The actor's job is not to perform the line.
The job is to test the theory.

The Socratic Actor Is Never Finished

A philosopher never stops asking.
Neither should an actor.

Even the smallest choices—posture, phrasing, rhythm—
reveal something profound when motivated by clarity.

And *why* is how we arrive at that clarity.

The Illusion of Depth

Actors love complexity.
We're taught to look for the "deep" reason.
To unearth trauma. To find the wound.
To chase an answer that feels big enough to justify the role.

But the truth is: depth often hides in plain sight.

1.   "I just wanted to be included."

2. "I was afraid they'd leave."

3. "I didn't know what else to do."

These aren't profound.
They're human.

And when spoken truthfully,
they don't need to be profound to be powerful.

What makes them feel deep is how they accumulate.
One simple *why* after another—
layered, reinforced, contradicted, revised—
until we see a life, not a line.

That's the essence of realism.

Not artifice.
Not invention.

Recognition.

So don't search for brilliance.
Search for what's honest.

Let the simple truths stack.
They'll take you somewhere complex.

Exercises:

Exercise 1: The Five Whys (Root Motive Drill)
Objective: Discover the emotional engine beneath an action.

Choose any action in the scene.
Ask why.
Take that answer—and ask why again.
Do this five times.

Debrief:
The final answer isn't an explanation.
It's fuel.
Now play the action with that fuel in your body.

Exercise 2: The Unstated Question
Objective: Surface subtext through inquiry.

For each line in a scene:

1. Write the *unstated why* behind it.

2. Then write the *question* the character is really asking.

Debrief:
How did this shape tone, rhythm, and breath?
What changed when the line became a question?

Exercise 3: Socratic Scene Analysis
Objective: Trace belief through behavior.

Take a short scene. For each action or choice, ask:
Why this, not something else?

Track the character's belief system—
What are they protecting?
What are they testing?
What are they trying not to know?

Debrief:
Does the character's strategy reveal their philosophy?
Where do they contradict themselves?

If the question is the actor's scalpel, the process that follows is where the real surgery happens. What follows is a companion method—my own toolset—for breaking a script open and becoming truly ready to perform

The Brownstone Script Analysis Tool

SECTION I: First Acquaintance — "The Read Without Need"

Before you ask questions, before you prepare—read it. Once. With no pen, no highlighter, no actor's brain. Let the scene wash over you like a dream you won't be allowed to remember.

Then ask:
- What stuck?
- What startled?
- What felt like me—and what didn't?

This is not analysis. It's orientation. A first hello. Don't dig. Don't interpret. Just listen.

SECTION II: Exploratory Construction — "Building the Illusion of Certainty"

Now that you've met the scene, start building understanding—but don't marry it. Use questions not as answers, but as scaffolding.

Suggested structure (to be filled out per scene):
1. What do I think this scene is about?
2. What do I want in the scene, and how do I chase it?
3. What tactics do I try, and when do they fail?
4. Where is the silence dangerous?
5. Which line feels the most unearned right now?

SECTION III: Destruction — "Ruin It on Purpose"

Once you've built the scene, tear it apart deliberately. Mistrust what you found. Question your emotional defaults.

Ask:
- What if the opposite were true?

- What if I lied in this line—intentionally or subconsciously?
- What happens if I make a terrible choice on purpose?
- What part of this is just my ego showing off?

Use this phase to break pattern recognition. The point isn't rebellion—it's re-calibration.

SECTION IV: Reconstruction — "The Craft of Readiness"

Now you've seen the scene from multiple angles, you're ready to rebuild without blueprint.

- Start running the scene without expectation.
- Don't "perform" it—just let it live inside tension.
- Every time you say a line, ask afterward: Did I believe that?
- Begin to listen with your skin, not your technique.

This is the stage where your imagination, your lived pressure, and the given circumstances fuse.

SECTION V: Throw It Away — And Mean It

Final preparation.

- Set aside the script.
- Don't run the scene again.
- Instead, run the moment before it begins. Let your body build tension.
- Say the first line only when it costs you something to say it.

By now, you know the scene so well you can forget it. And when you forget it honestly—you're ready to find it again, for real, in the moment.

SECTION VI: Interrogating the Line — "Why This, Not That?"

This is not about interpretation. It's about intimacy.

The deeper your relationship to the exact words on the page, the less you'll need to "act."

Ask this for every sentence, clause, or phrase:
- Why this phrasing, not another?
- What word surprises me—or feels like a clue?
- Where is the subject placed? The verb? What does that say about urgency or control?
- If I changed this word, what emotional or tonal shift would that cause?

By unpacking each line this way, you aren't "figuring out" how to say it. You're removing the need to figure it out at all.

SECTION VII: Anti-Context Drills — "Unseat the Obvious"

Most scenes come with built-in expectations. Actors rush to inhabit the obvious. The result? Predictable work.

Choose 3 "wrong" contexts and rehearse your scene within them:
- A prison confrontation in a British garden
- A love confession during a hostage crisis
- A goodbye between friends set in a courtroom

Ask:
- What behavior emerges?
- What images or rhythms surprise me?
- What do I notice about the real scene when I return to it?

This is not to change your setting on the day—it's to undo the limitations your assumptions impose.

SECTION VIII: Emotional Truth — "Sensation Before Sentiment"

You are not here to feel for the character. You are here to become a vessel in which the character might feel.

The emotion is not your job. The conditions are your job.

By using psychological gesture (à la Chekhov), we let the body lead. The body generates emotional possibility, not performance.

Try this:
- Identify a single gesture that captures the character's dominant condition.
- Expand it physically. Let it take over your spine, face, breath.
- Now reduce it to a fingertip, an inhale, a glance.
- Carry that residue into the scene.

This is not "playing a mood." It's setting the emotional climate in which the scene happens.

Compare this to emotional recall:
- It depletes the actor
- It collapses over time
- It treats the actor's history as the source, not the character's world

Actors like Daniel Day-Lewis, Christian Bale, and Jeremy Strong—while often labeled "method"—are not regurgitating past wounds. They are pursuing an unreachable synthesis. Cate Blanchett has spoken about doing mountains of preparation, then throwing it all away the moment she steps on set. Why? Because the audience doesn't want to see your process—they want to see life. You won't become the character. But if you commit to this process, the character may start becoming something that could only exist through you.

Chapter Thirteen: Action Without Stakes Is Dead

Lines are not the performance.
Stakes are.

Most actors approach the work like they're building a statue.
Once it's chiseled into place—done.
That's the character.
That's the "performance."
Locked.

But screen acting will break that kind of thinking.

Because in film and television, you don't get to live your role in order.
You don't even always get to finish a thought before you have to reset for sound.
You shoot Episode 4 before Episode 1.
You shoot the breakup before the first kiss.
You shoot the death before the love even blooms.

The performance doesn't move in a straight line.
So the actor can't either.

This is the discipline of long-term character work:
to build a role that remains alive across time, context, and chaos.

The Character Is Never Done

If you're trying to "find" your character once and for all, you're already dead.
The character isn't an object you construct and then protect.
It's a relationship.
It evolves.
It deepens.
It contradicts itself.

And thank God for that.

If the character's choices are locked in by your prep, how do you leave space for surprise?

For discovery?
For instinct?

You don't need to "solve" the role.
You need to stay in relationship with it.
To wake up next to it.
To ask, "Who are you today?"
And to listen for the answer—even when it's not what you expected.

Actors often try to lock in a version of the character early.
That's fear talking.
Let it go.

The best work comes when you build from openness and imaginative readiness,
not "clarity" or performance polish.

Organic Evolution vs. Fossilized Performance

Repetition is part of the job.
So is out-of-sequence shooting.

The danger is that, to survive that structure, actors cling to choices they made early—
safe ones, shallow ones—just to keep the performance "consistent."

But consistency without growth is death.

This is where your embodied technique matters.
Archetypal gesture.
Psychological gesture.
Objective.
Stakes.

If those remain alive, the performance will remain alive.
But if you're relying on a "take" you rehearsed weeks ago,
you're acting a memory—not the moment.

Your job is not to remember how you did it.
It's to live it again, every time.

Not identically—
honestly.

Tracking the Arc Without Forcing It

Let's say you're in a 10-episode arc.
You know your character starts selfish and ends vulnerable.
Great.

But you don't get to play that arc in order.
So how do you build it?

You build it like a novelist.
With notes.
With maps.
With questions.

Ask:
"What has this character learned up to this scene?"

Not what they will learn.
Not where they'll end.
Just—what's present right now.

Track internal shifts scene-by-scene.
Not to perform the change—
but to understand the internal resistance.

Most change is invisible until it's complete.
Let that truth inform how your character clings to their old way of being—
even as something new begins to crack underneath.

The audience won't track the arc through your "performance of change."
They'll feel it leaking out of the seams.

Re-Entering the Role (After a Break)

You shot Episode 3 last spring.
Now it's fall, and they've rewritten Episode 7.

How do you get back in?

Not with your head.
With your body.

Go back to the movement.
The breath.
The gestures.
The pace of the character's thoughts.
The way they sit.
The way they enter a room.

Read a scene aloud and track what words the character avoids.
What moments they resist.
What silences cost them something.

If your prep was embodied, your return will be instinctual.
If it wasn't, you'll be searching for a costume that no longer fits.

The Actor's Journal

The work is surgical.
This is tactical..

Track what your character fears.
What they fantasize about.
What physical sensations dominate their body.

Keep a sensory archive.
Sketch images.
Write dreams as if they're the character's.
Track colors, sounds, seasons, symbols.

This work is non-linear.
You're building a well you can draw from across months—maybe years.

Let your prep be intuitive, but organized.
You're creating a living history of a fictional life.

Collaborating Without Compromise

Long-term roles often mean multiple directors, rewrites, tone shifts, and external notes.

The danger is you become a translator—
just trying to please everyone and keep your version intact.

But you don't serve the story by defending old choices.
You serve it by adapting truthfully.

Ask:
"How does this rewrite affect what the character wants?"
Not:
"Does this contradict what I planned?"

Let directors lead you into new rooms—without abandoning what the character already owns.

The flexibility isn't weakness.
It's strength.

Your job is to evolve without shattering.

You're not protecting a performance.
You're midwifing a person.

Final Note: You Don't Need to Get It Right

That's the myth.

That you need to figure it all out.
Lock it in.

Preserve it.
"Stay consistent."

But consistency is what ruins actors.

What you need is aliveness.

A living character doesn't repeat.
They return.
They re-enter.
They shift.

The job is not to preserve the role.
The job is to let it keep growing.

Exercises:

Exercise 1: The Fragment Map
Objective: Track your character's evolving state across non-linear scenes.

1. Choose three scenes from different points in the story.
2. For each, answer:
    1. What does my character want?
    2. What do they fear?
    3. What are they refusing to admit?
3. Create a visual or written "map" of these emotional fragments.

Debrief:
Which parts of your character stay consistent?
Which evolve?
What new questions arise?

Exercise 2: Re-Entering the Role

Objective: Return to a character after time away.

1. Read a short scene as your character, focusing only on behavior, not tone.

2. Use gesture, breath, or walk to re-locate the character's physical rhythm.

3. Journal for five minutes in the character's voice, as if they're reflecting on what just happened.

Debrief:

What physical or emotional memory helped you reconnect?
Did you discover anything you didn't know the first time around?

Chapter Fourteen: A New Pedagogy — Philosophy, Imagination, and the Body

If the old ways collapse under pressure, then it's time to build something that doesn't.

The modern actor faces a paradox:
More content than ever—yet fewer tools that truly liberate.

We live in a golden age of performance, yet traditional pedagogy still clings to the bones of a broken machine—one that prizes mimicry over meaning, and memory over imagination.

The time has come to build something better.
Something that reflects the real demands of screen work, and the real needs of the modern artist.

What follows is not a prescribed method.
It is a framework—a new pedagogy grounded in three central tenets: philosophy, imagination, and the body.

Each one challenges the actor to rethink not just how they perform, but how they prepare.

---

1. Philosophy — The Actor as Questioner

Acting is not mere imitation.
It is investigation.

The actor must evolve into a philosopher of performance—interrogating the text, the character, and even the nature of self-expression itself.

Instead of beginning with fixed answers, the process starts with asking real, penetrating questions:

1. What is the function of this story?

2. What is this character revealing—or refusing to reveal?

3. What must the audience feel or understand by the end of this scene?

Historical figures serve as guiding lights.

Plato's Allegory of the Cave reminds us not to accept mere shadows, but to inquire about their source.
Shakespeare, with his insistence that the actor "hold the mirror up to nature," reminds us that performance is not passive reflection—it is active engagement with hidden truths.

In this framework, the actor is not a vessel for pre-packaged emotion.
They are a vessel-breaker.
They dare to expose what others would rather keep hidden.

Modern directors—and even celebrated method actors who evolved beyond their early techniques—underscore this:
Genuine performance begins not with reproducing a script, but with questioning the given circumstances at every turn.

---

2. Imagination — The Engine of Empathy and Adaptability

The actor who cannot imagine cannot act—at least not truthfully, and not sustainably.

This framework distinguishes between passive and active imagination:

1. Passive imagination is involuntary: anxiety spirals, unbidden memories, fantasies at 3 a.m.

2. Active imagination is deliberate: the conscious construction of environments, stakes, and inner realities.

Training the actor's active imagination is non-negotiable.

Modern screen actors like Viola Davis and Joaquin Phoenix have spoken about how actively building sensory environments—even in a minimal set—enables them to find emotional truth.

Active imagination is a muscle.
On film, where rehearsal time is rare and conditions shift without warning, active imagination becomes not a luxury—but a survival skill.

It is how performance remains alive inside an ever-changing reality.

---

3. The Body — The First Place Where Truth Appears

If imagination is the spark,
the body is the fuse.

This pedagogy moves beyond emotional recall or personal biography—and returns to the body as the site where truth first manifests.

Michael Chekhov understood this:
"The body knows before the brain does."

Preparation begins not with remembering emotion, but with shaping posture, rhythm, gesture, breath.

Modern research on embodied cognition supports this:
Physical stance affects emotional state.
Confidence expands breath.
Fear contracts posture.
Grief slows pace.

In screen acting, where every flicker of movement matters, physical truth communicates what dialogue often cannot.

This framework asks:
Can you inhabit the character's physical reality fully, even before you "feel" it?

The goal is not relatability.
The goal is embodied resonance.

The Framework in Action

Traditional training has often collapsed into mining personal memory.

But overemphasis on emotional recall traps actors in repetition—and drains adaptability.

This new framework calls for balance:
Integrating philosophical inquiry, active imaginative creation, and embodied preparation.

Modern performances that feel fluid, spontaneous, and alive—despite chaotic filming conditions—are rarely accidents.
They result from this kind of dynamic, multi-dimensional preparation.

Actors conditioned this way do not cling to a single "perfect" performance.
They remain open.
Responsive.
Elastic.

They replace fear with readiness.
They replace mimicry with meaning.

They are not simply acting.
They are bearing witness.

Conclusion

This new pedagogy does not guarantee a flawless performance.
It offers something better:

A framework that empowers the actor to meet the unpredictable demands of modern screen work—and survive them truthfully.

It asks:
"What truth is trying to be seen here?"
And it demands that truth emerge not from perfection, but from presence.

By training philosophy, imagination, and the body as equal forces, the actor transforms not just their craft—but the experience of the audience itself.

They make every performance a revelation of life's deeper, often unseen dimensions.

But technique alone is not enough.
Skill without direction is just noise.

To truly matter now, the actor must understand the responsibility that comes with these tools—
the demand to bear witness,
to reveal,
to break through a culture built on illusion.

That is the work we turn to next.

Exercises:

Exercise 1: Stake the Scene Higher
Objective: Practice raising stakes and responding truthfully.

1. Choose a mundane domestic scene (e.g., roommates arguing over dishes).

2. Assign new internal stakes:
    1. One character is about to leave forever.
    2. One character is hiding a major illness.
3. Play the same lines with the new stakes alive underneath.

Debrief:
What shifted in behavior, intention, or tension?
Did the mundane become urgent?

Exercise 2: Philosophy into Practice
Objective: Integrate philosophical questioning into performance preparation.

1. Choose a short two-person scene with emotional stakes.
2. Before rehearsal, each actor answers in writing:
    1. What truth is trying to be seen in this scene?
    2. What part of this truth is difficult or uncomfortable to face?
    3. What does this moment ask of the audience—emotionally, ethically, spiritually?
3. Re-approach the scene with these questions living underneath, fueling behavior—not as exposition, but as active subtext.

Debrief:
What shifted between versions?
Did the deeper inquiry affect rhythm, stakes, or physicality?
How did philosophical intention guide the imagination and body differently than traditional "choices"?

Chapter Fifteen: The Actor's Responsibility

We are living through an era of illusion.

The line between authenticity and performance has blurred.
Politicians perform sincerity.
Influencers monetize vulnerability.
Brands manufacture empathy.
Everyone is acting.

In this climate, the actor's responsibility has never been more urgent.
Not to blend in.
But to break through.
To remind us what real truth feels like when it's not for sale.

Performance Is Now the Currency of Power

We are surrounded by experts in simulation—executives, public figures, even algorithms.
Every gesture, pause, and smile is curated.

But these performances don't reveal.
They persuade.

They manufacture the feeling of sincerity without the risk of actually being seen.

The professional actor must stand in contrast.
While others use performance to manipulate, we must use it to reveal.

The difference isn't stylistic.
It's moral.

When a social media influencer cries on camera, it's often calibrated.
When Viola Davis weeps in *Fences* or Riz Ahmed shatters in *Sound of Metal*, it's something else entirely.

It's an offering, not an extraction.
It's connection, not transaction.

Acting Is a Compass, Not an Escape

Great acting doesn't distract us from the world's chaos.
It shows us how to find meaning inside it.

It gives shape to grief, hope, contradiction.
It makes choices visible again.

In a world of noise, feeling becomes possible again through art.

Call it a luxury if you want—
but without it, the work fails.

You Are a Witness

You are not here to perform perfection.
You are here to embody the unspeakable.

The actor's work is to consecrate space for things a culture refuses to name.

That is a political act.
That is a spiritual act.

Because when a society stops feeling, it starts breaking.

Presence Is Revolutionary

In an age of distraction, mere presence becomes radical.

You are not training to perform a character.
You are training to remain undeniable—

to inhabit each breath so completely that the audience is forced to come with you.

Not to impress.
But to see.
And to make seen.

Acting Is a Moral Act

Attention is the currency of our era.
And you, as an actor, control what happens once you have it.

Your work shapes what people believe is valid, what they dare to feel, and what possibilities they can imagine.

That is a heavy responsibility.
It is also an extraordinary gift.

This Is the Charge

Don't be the most polished actor in the room.
Be the one who risks the most.

Be the one who breathes when others freeze.
Be the one who lets silence linger until it becomes undeniable.

Be the one who reminds the world what it's like to feel something that isn't for sale.

The world doesn't need another illusion.
It needs you.

Whole.
Present.
Brave.

Fallible.
True.

Exercises:

Exercise 1: The Story I Must Tell
Objective: Connect acting choices to personal and social meaning.

1. Reflect on a truth or experience you feel compelled to share.

2. Choose or write a monologue that gives voice to that experience.

3. Perform it not as a performance—but as a testimony.

Debrief:
What changed when the work became personal?
How did intention shift the energy of the performance?

Exercise 2: The Lie in the Line
Objective: Dismantle performative falseness.

1. Choose a scene or monologue where the character is pretending ("I'm fine," "I don't care," etc.).

2. Perform it twice:

    1. First, playing the external lie.

    2. Second, letting the real feeling leak through underneath.

Debrief:
What was revealed when the surface cracked?
How did vulnerability change the audience's experience?

Chapter Sixteen: A Tale of Two Tightropes

Freedom without responsibility collapses into noise.
It's time to aim it at something that matters.
And once you aim it, you must walk it.

There's a piece of advice actors hear all the time—especially from casting directors who've become coaches:

"You're not booking because you're not making big, bold choices."

What they mean is often true.
But what the actor hears is something else entirely.

They hear:
Be louder.
Be quirkier.
Do something unexpected.
Add a flourish.
Make it pop.

And so they start tap-dancing.
Metaphorically, and sometimes literally.
They rehearse "boldness" as behavior, instead of conviction.
They mistake size for substance.
They choreograph tricks instead of cultivating truth.

This misunderstanding leads to one of the most dangerous habits in the audition room:
the two-foot tightrope.

The Two-Foot Tightrope

Too many actors rehearse like they're walking a tightrope that's only two feet off the ground.
They craft clever bits.
Memorize affectations.
Polish delivery.

They rehearse the safest version of boldness—one that can survive the fall if it fails.

But the real performance—the one that books the job, the one that changes the room—
is not found on that rope.

The One That Matters

The real tightrope—the one that matters—is 100 feet in the air.

There is no net.
There is no choreographed routine.
There is only wind.
And you.

That wind is the partner's unexpected line.
It's the last-minute rewrite.
It's the shift in tone, or blocking, or circumstance.
It's the thing you didn't prepare for—and must meet anyway.

And when it comes, you cannot freeze.
You cannot recite your "bold choice."
You cannot hold your breath and hope they don't notice you're scared.

You must walk.
You must feel the rope, not force it.
You must respond.
Not perform.
Not protect.
Respond.

The Real Definition of Bold

A bold choice isn't loud.
A bold choice is alive.

It breathes.
It risks.
It listens.
It lets itself be changed.

And it only works if you've trained for something deeper than behavior.

Preparation That Survives the Fall

Actors who rehearse for a perfect moment are always shocked when that moment doesn't arrive.

But actors who prepare for impact—who prepare for the rope to shake, for the wind to howl—are ready.

This is the heart of a new pedagogy:

1. You train the body so it knows how to walk in any wind.
2. You train the imagination so you can see the world even when the set is blank.
3. You train philosophy so you can understand the why behind the walk.

And then you let the scene change you.

That's not just artistry.
That's discipline.
That's freedom.

The Dangerous Confusion

When actors are told to make big, bold choices, what casting often means is:

We want to see you commit.
To risk.
To take a stand.

But what actors often do instead is fabricate eccentricity.
They layer on behavior instead of stripping down to truth.
And then they wonder why no one believes them.

The truth is:
A character making a terrifying phone call with stillness and breath is a bolder choice than an actor adding "business" with a coffee cup to look busy.

The boldest thing you can do is feel the risk—and walk anyway.

Walk It, Don't Prove It

You don't need to show us your balance.
You just need to keep walking.

Let the rope shake.
Let the wind blow.
Let yourself not know what's next.

If your preparation is alive, you will be too.

Exercises:

Exercise 1: Prepare for the Unknown
Objective: Train the body and imagination to stay alive when the scene shifts unexpectedly.

1. Choose a scene you know well—something memorized and rehearsed.

2. Perform the scene once as prepared.

3. Then have a partner (or coach) introduce unpredictable changes while you perform:

    1. Skip or alter a line.

    2. Change the emotional tone.

    3. Interrupt with a question or unexpected physical gesture.

    4. Give a last-minute direction ("Now you're freezing cold," "Now you're late for a flight").

4. Without stopping, stay in the moment and respond truthfully to the changes.

Debrief:
Did you cling to the original plan, or allow yourself to adapt?
Where did you freeze?
Where did you let the rope move beneath you?
What tools helped you stay alive inside the scene rather than retreating to performance?

Exercise 2: Stillness Under Risk
Objective: Strengthen conviction and emotional presence without layering on false behavior.

1. Choose a monologue or short scene with high emotional stakes (confession, confrontation, loss).

2. Perform it once using any natural physical behaviors (gestures, pacing, props).

3. Then perform it again under a new constraint:

    1. No physical movement allowed except essential breath, eye movement, and vocal shifts.

4. Focus all your risk into stillness—feeling the stakes internally, without "showing" it through activity.

Debrief:
Did stillness make the emotional risk feel bigger or smaller?
Did you feel more or less truthful without "proving" your emotions?
How did the audience's experience change when you stopped demonstrating and simply walked the emotional tightrope?

Chapter Seventeen: To Action — To Throw It Away and Mean It

Survival on the rope is only the beginning.
Now you must learn to aim each step—each gesture—with precision and purpose.

Action is the DNA of performance.
It transforms lines into meaning, movement into motive, presence into pressure.
And yet for many actors, actioning has become either a prescriptive exercise or an abandoned tool—something scribbled in a notebook, never lived in the body.

This is where we reclaim it.

Action Is Not a Trick — It's a Muscle

When I was first taught actions, they were precise.
Not broad verbs like "to tease" or "to threaten,"
but textured motivations:
"to dangle a ball of yarn in front of a cat."
Not "to seduce," but "to draw someone in like a tide pulling a boat."

The goal wasn't to memorize an action per line.
The goal was to live the truth that every line and every gesture carries intent.

And the only way to live that truth—moment to moment—is to train for it.
Until action becomes instinct, not ornament.

Archetypal Gesture as Gateway to Action

To begin this training, I use a modified version of Michael Chekhov's Archetypal Gesture.

Seven primary physical actions:

To Place

To Lift

To Throw

To Drag

To Push

To Pull

To Rip

Why seven?
Because seven is intuitive.
Seven character questions.
Seven digits in a phone number.
Seven fits the mind's rhythm.

These gestures are not ends.
They are beginnings—containers for more specific behavior.

"To Place" could mean setting down a teacup with trembling care—
or laying divorce papers on the bed like a death sentence.

"To Rip" could be shredding a contract—or breaking a heart.

Specificity emerges through modification.

Breaking Down "Just Throw It Away"

Let's take a ubiquitous piece of direction:
"Just throw it away."

We know what it means intuitively.
But let's break it down:

Action Verb: To throw. (But not just any throw—context matters.)

Modifier: Away. Disposal. Separation.

Quality: Just — suggesting ease, dismissal, emotional detachment.

So what the director is really asking is:

Discard it with effortless separation.

And even that discarding could be cruel, casual, tired, or tender.

It's still an action.
Still a choice.

When you break it down, you stop playing generalities—and start aiming your performance with purpose.

Why This Matters

When you learn to action—even at a granular, physical level—you understand the engine beneath the language.

You stop performing lines.
You start doing something.

And once you know how to do, you can stop scripting and start living.

Experienced actors may not sit down and "action" every scene consciously.
But if you asked them mid-shoot, "What are you doing here?"—they would have an answer.

That answer isn't memorized.
It's trained.

We're not here to float through text.
We're here to shape it.
To aim it.
To throw it.
And sometimes—yes—to throw it away.

Exercises:

Exercise 1: Archetypal Action Rehearsal

Objective: Connect physical gesture to psychological action.

Choose a short scene or monologue.

Assign one archetypal action (e.g., To Push).

Rehearse the scene while physically exploring that action's variations:

What kind of push? Gentle, desperate, explosive?

What's resisting you?

What's at stake if you fail?

Debrief:
What emerged when action preceded text?
Did the gesture unlock clarity, conflict, or new emotional weight?

Exercise 2: Break It Down

Objective: Deconstruct vague directions into specific actionable components.

Choose common phrases like:

"Throw it away."

"Push it harder."

"Let it go."

Break each into:

Action Verb

Modifier (object, direction, target)

Quality (tone, intensity)

Apply that action structure consciously to a moment in a scene.

Debrief:
How did specificity shift performance?
Did clearer intent surface new emotions or unexpected tension?

Chapter Eighteen: Take After Take

In theater, you rehearse for weeks.
You build rhythm, timing, ensemble.
You find the scene's emotional wave and ride it again and again.

On set, you might get one blocking rehearsal—
then six takes from three angles under completely different conditions.

And you're expected to be just as real.
Just as spontaneous.
Just as precise.

This is the paradox of screen acting:

You must repeat without repeating.

The Trap of Consistency

Actors often try to solve this problem by remembering what they did:

1. *"I cried on that line in Take 2."*

2. *"I put the cup down right before I turned."*

3. *"I sighed before I said it last time—should I do it again?"*

That's not acting.
That's choreography.

And worse—it's fragile.

If the other actor changes their timing…
If the editor cuts away before your cue…
If the lighting rig squeals in the middle of your close-up…

You're unmoored.
You're not in the scene.
You're trying to match a memory.

The pursuit of external consistency kills internal life.

Emotion Isn't a Pose

Real emotion doesn't loop.
It evolves.

You can't "do what you did before."
Because what you did before was a result—not a plan.

The tear wasn't a choice.
It was a symptom of something alive.

Trying to copy it is like mimicking a sneeze.
It's always artificial.

Instead of repeating the behavior—carry the sensation.

Let the body remember what it felt like.
Not to cry.
But to need something.
To fear something.
To protect something.

That's what made the moment real in the first place.

The Performance Is Not Yours

This is the uncomfortable truth of screen acting:

You don't own the take.

The performance is built later—
out of fragments, sound bytes, pickups, inserts, reactions.

Sometimes, the moment that lands isn't the one you felt was best—
it's the one that cut together best.

So stop trying to control the result.

Instead, make each take:

1. Truthful.

2. Alive.

3. Rooted.

Let the editor choose which truth the story needs.

Repetition as Evolution

The best actors don't give six identical takes.
They give six **truthful** takes.

Each one slightly different.
Each one shaped by the moment.

Sometimes quieter.
Sometimes messier.
Sometimes more still.

But never dead.
Never locked.

They're not chasing consistency.
They're chasing **integrity**.

Think Like a Musician

A great jazz musician doesn't replay the same solo verbatim.

They return to the theme—
and improvise within it.

Each take is a new conversation,
not a reprint.

Actors must do the same.

You know your objective.
You've prepared the stakes.
You've embodied the character's rhythm.

Now speak it again—for the first time.

Exercises:

Exercise 1: The Loop Without Mimicry
Objective: Rehearse variation through shifting attention.

Choose a high-stakes moment from a scene. Repeat it 5–6 times, back to back. Shift your attention each time:

1. Once to what just happened

2. Once to what you're trying to prevent

3. Once to the other actor's eyes

4. Once to what you're hiding

Debrief:
Notice what changed—without forcing anything.
Each take is honest, but different.

Exercise 2: Anchor the Sensation, Not the Behavior
Objective: Reconnect emotion through body memory.
Setup:
Identify the emotional engine of a moment.
Where did you feel it? Chest? Gut? Jaw?

Breathe into that place.

Now do the scene again—not copying behavior, but using that **bodily sensation** as your anchor.

Debrief:
Did the emotion return on its own?
Did the body guide you toward new discoveries?

Chapter Nineteen: Acting as Sport

We don't watch sports for the plot.
We watch for the performance.

We watch to see what a human being does under pressure—
how their skill holds up when the stakes are real.
How they adapt.
How they collapse.
How they rise.

That's why people will still watch actors in an age of AI.

Not because the story demands it.
But because performance is witnessed, not simulated.
It is a human act.
Under human tension.
Executed in real time, with real consequences.

The Art of Execution

Most acting books treat the craft like therapy or philosophy.
And yes, it can be both.

But on set, no one's asking how you feel about your childhood.
They're asking if you're ready.
If you can take direction.
If you can deliver—again and again—under moving lights and last-minute rewrites, without losing the thread.

That's not just art.
That's athleticism.

Pressure Makes It Real

You can feel the pressure on set—even if no one talks about it.

Time is money.

There's no rehearsal.

You're meeting your scene partner five minutes before rolling.

The shot is tight. The boom is just outside frame.

Someone flubs their line. The tension breaks. Now you have to summon it again. And again.

This is performance under duress.

And the audience doesn't care what the conditions were.
They only see the result.

Like a gymnast landing a routine, or a pitcher delivering under stadium lights—
your job is to deliver when it counts.

Not perfectly.
But truthfully.

Craft Is What Survives Chaos

Raw talent gets you into the room.
Craft is what survives once the room falls apart.

Craft is what keeps you grounded when the lights go out,
the camera rolls late,
or your cue is missed.

Craft is how you recover between takes.
Craft is how you access a moment on the fourth setup,
three hours later,
with half the crew watching and a leaf blower outside.

This is why athletes train fundamentals.
Not for when things go right.
For when they don't.

Actors must do the same.

The Rehearsal Room Is the Gym

Training is not sacred.
It's practical.

It's where you strengthen the tools you'll need when things break down.

You rehearse not to preserve a perfect version of the scene—
but to increase your adaptability when the version you imagined falls apart.

You build stamina.
Reflex.
Breathing.
Clarity.

You test your limits so they don't break on set.

The actor's body is their engine.
The text is their terrain.
The camera is the weather.
And the work is the race.

Why Sports Will Never Be Replaced — And Why Acting Won't Either

No one watches sports for the outcome alone—
except degenerate gamblers, and they don't care what this chapter is about.

The point isn't what happened.
It's how it happened.

We watch because we admire the human behind the performance.
Because we know—from our own body—how hard it is to do what they're doing.

To sink the shot.
To stick the landing.
To hold focus when thousands are watching.

That's what makes sports meaningful.
And the same is true for acting.

You don't need to be an actor to admire acting.
You just need to have felt heartbreak.
Shame.
Desire.
Anger.

You just need to have tried to be honest—
and know how hard that is.

That's why people still watch real actors.

Because we know, deep down, what it costs to stay honest under pressure.
And because we want to believe someone can do it.

Why AI Can't Compete

AI might simulate behavior.
But it doesn't carry risk.
It doesn't struggle.
It doesn't recover.

It can mimic pain, but it cannot survive it.
It can replicate subtlety, but it cannot earn it.

It can loop a perfect emotional arc—
but it can't mean it.

And human beings know the difference.
Because we know what real effort looks like.

We know when something was done well versus generated.
We feel it in the breath.
In the timing.
In the vulnerability.

Just like in sport.

We watch because someone is doing something difficult—
and they're doing it for us.

Acting Has Survived Every Technological Threat

This isn't the first time someone said actors were finished.

They said it when animation exploded.
Why use actors when you can draw characters bigger, faster, funnier?

They said it during the rise of reality TV.
Who needs scripted work when real people can be filmed for free?

They said it when CGI and motion capture became cheap.
Why hire someone to perform when you can build a flawless avatar?

They said it again when digital cameras and YouTube made content accessible to anyone.

And now they're saying it with AI.

And yet—actors remain.

Because audiences don't just want a story.
They want to watch someone *do* it.

They want to see:

The timing.

The risk.

The failure.

The recovery.

The craft.

That hasn't changed.
And it won't.

Because performance is not a product.
It's a human event.

Like sport.

We admire what's hard.
We recognize what's real.

And we still believe in the skill it takes to do it truthfully—
take after take,
breath after breath,
moment after moment.

Acting doesn't survive because we protect it.
It survives because we still recognize what's real—
and what it costs.

Exercises:

Exercise 1: The Clock Is Ticking
Objective: Practice truthful spontaneity under time pressure.

Give yourself 60 seconds of prep.
No script. No context.
Just an objective and a single line.

Deliver it.

Repeat three times with new imaginary circumstances.

Debrief:
Did the pressure help or hinder clarity?
What changed when you had less time to prepare?

Exercise 2: Start in Chaos
Objective: Build emotional focus amid distraction.

Rehearse a monologue while performing a distracting physical task (jumping jacks, cleaning, pacing).

Then snap into focus and deliver the scene on cue.

Debrief:
Could you find your center under duress?
How quickly could you shift into the emotional life?

Exercise 3: The Recovery Drill
Objective: Practice in-scene resilience.

Have a partner interrupt your scene at random:

Line flubs

Missed cues

Unexpected shifts

Your task: recover.
Stay present.
Keep the stakes alive.

Debrief:
What grounded you?
What tools helped you stay connected despite the disruption?

Chapter Twenty: The Lineage of Liberation

You've been challenged to see acting differently—
not as imitation, but as action.
Not as self-expression, but as revelation.
And if you've taken that challenge seriously,
then you're already standing at the edge of something larger.
Because this isn't just technique.
It's inheritance.
You are stepping into a lineage of artists who refused to settle for shadows.

We Began in the Cave

Not Plato's, exactly—but one like it.
A space where actors were taught to reflect reality without questioning it.
To recreate behavior instead of illuminating meaning.
To disappear behind the curtain of naturalism—and call it truth.

We've walked out of that cave now.
We've looked at the flame.
Felt the heat.
Seen what casts the shadow.

We've turned away from methods that reduce us to our memories—
and turned toward a practice that elevates our purpose.

We've remembered what great actors have always known:

Truth doesn't live in imitation.
It lives in the doing.

This Is Not a Method—It's a Mirror

This book has not offered a method.
It has offered a mirror—

a way to see where we've been,
and where we might go.

A mirror not to flatten, but to frame.
To aim with precision.
To wield with purpose.

And in doing so, it joins a lineage of teachers and thinkers who never stopped asking better questions:

1. Michael Chekhov showed us that gesture is the doorway to emotional truth.

2. Viola Spolin reminded us that play is sacred.

3. Jerzy Grotowski stripped theatre bare to find what could not be faked.

4. Uta Hagen grounded us in action.

5. Kristin Linklater gave voice to breath and body.

6. Anne Bogart mapped the architecture of time and space.

7. Stella Adler returned the world to the actor.

8. Sanford Meisner taught us that listening is an act of love.

These weren't gurus.
They were liberators.

And their work didn't replace the past—it reinterpreted it.
It dared to move forward.

This Is Your Inheritance

This is your inheritance.
And your charge.

To act not as a mirror of reality,
but as a shaper of meaning.

To hold that mirror up not passively—
but deliberately.

To show virtue her own feature.
Scorn her own image.
And the age its form and pressure.

Because the world is full of illusion.
And the actor—at their best—is the one who reminds us how it feels to see clearly.

That's the revolution.

Thank you for walking it with me.

The Lineage Is Alive

This lineage is not an artifact.
It is a living inheritance.
And it demands more from us now than ever before.

We are the next stewards.
We are the ones who must protect what cannot be digitized,
cannot be faked,
cannot be flattened into imitation.

We must not only honor what they gave us—
we must evolve it to survive the storm that is already here.

And that begins by facing the new world for what it is.

The task of the actor has never been simply to imitate life.
It has always been to see beyond the shadows—
and to shape what meaning can still be made from them.

That task is more urgent now than ever.

Epilogue: The Last Undeniable Thing — Acting in a Manufactured World

By the time you reach this point, you've seen the cracks—
in the tradition, in the training, in the assumptions we make about what acting is and how it works.

But behind all of it is a deeper crisis.
One that goes beyond performance technique or style.
The crisis of meaning itself.

We are living in a world where reality is increasingly manufactured.

Faces can be fabricated.
Emotions simulated.
Performances stitched together from data.

The acting profession—especially on screen—is facing a threat it has never encountered before:
the loss of its human center.

And this isn't theoretical.
It's happening now.

Actors are being scanned.
Voices cloned.
Scenes assembled without real interaction.
Entire shows written, cast, and rendered with minimal human input.

The machine has learned how to look real.
But it doesn't mean anything.
And it never will.

The Line We Stand On

This is the line we stand on.

If we allow ourselves to become imitators—
copying behaviors, mimicking reactions, offering polished

simulations—
we will train ourselves into irrelevance.

We will be indistinguishable from code.

But realism, as we've reclaimed it here, offers another way forward.

Realism is not reproduction.
It is interpretation.

It is the actor's responsibility to shape reality—
not mirror it.
To find meaning where none is obvious.
To embody contradiction.
To wrestle with uncertainty.

To stand in front of the lens, not just as a character,
but as a human being engaged in the dangerous act of revealing truth.

That truth may be incomplete.
It may be ecstatic.
It may be brutal.
But it cannot be faked.

The body knows when something is real.
The imagination knows when something matters.
And the audience, when they see it, knows too.

The Actor's Responsibility Now

This is the actor's responsibility now:

To become the last undeniable thing
in a world increasingly built to feel safe, shallow, and synthetic.

To make art not by imitating life, but by risking it.
By stepping into the unknown—
with a trained body, an awakened imagination,
and the courage to bring something into the world that no algorithm can replicate.

That's why we train.
That's why we tell stories.
That's why acting still matters.

Because machines can replicate behavior.
But only humans can wrest meaning from the void.

And that is the work.
That is the fire.
That is the truth.

Final Chapter: Hating the Waiting — Resilience in the Age of Delay

You've done everything right.
You've trained.
Prepared.
Taped.
Submitted.

You've been told you're "close."
That they "loved your tape."
That you're "on the radar."

And still—
nothing.

Not a no.
Not a yes.
Just the hum of quiet inboxes and calendars that don't fill.

This is not rejection.
It's suspension.
And it wears you down.

The Industry Runs on Delay

No one talks about it.
But delay is built into the system.

Projects fall apart.
Casting shifts.
Budgets stall.
Your best work is often met with silence, not resistance.

It's not about doing something wrong.
It's about waiting on something that wasn't built to see you clearly.
The machine is slow, indecisive, and indifferent by design.

 And it takes a toll.

"Be Patient" Isn't the Answer

You're not being impatient.
You're being human.

You've built momentum.
You've sacrificed stability.
You've trained to be ready—
and now you're waiting for permission to be seen.

"Be patient" sounds wise.
But in this context, it's a dismissal.

What you need isn't patience.
What you need is a plan.

Survival Isn't Passive

Real patience isn't silence.
It's persistence.

It's rehearsal without applause.
Discipline without a deadline.
Art without approval.

It's knowing that your value isn't validated by booking—
it's proven by consistency.

And yes, that's hard to believe when nothing is happening.

But **this is where careers are built**—
not in the spotlight,
but in the space between spotlights.

The Pain of "Almost"

Being told you're close can break you.

You replay every moment of the tape,
every beat of the audition.
You start to doubt your instincts.
You question your trajectory.
You wonder if you've misread everything.

You haven't.

You're just feeling the cost of caring.
And that's what makes you an artist.

It's not weakness.
It's the cost of staying awake

Make the Waiting Work for You

You don't control the timing.
But you control the *truth* of what you build while you wait.

You rehearse anyway.
You write anyway.
You mentor. You study. You perform in a classroom or a hallway or your kitchen.

Because acting isn't what happens when you get the job.
It's what you do when no one is watching.

That's where your muscles form.
That's where your voice sharpens.
That's where you remember who you are.

No One Will Save You

There is no "break" coming to rescue you.
No perfect role to justify the journey.

What comes is the next chance.
The next shot.
And you don't know when.

So you prepare.

Not to stay busy.
But to stay *ready*.

And in staying ready, you regain control.

You're not waiting.
You're *building*.

You're Not Delusional

The world may not reflect your value yet.
But that doesn't mean it's not real.

You are not crazy for still believing in what you can do.

You are not wasting time by staying in the game.

You are not wrong to want it—
deeply, fully, entirely.

This frustration you feel?
It's the evidence that you haven't given up.

And that matters more than anything.

Exercises:

Exercise 1: The Unseen Log
Objective: Track invisible progress.

For one week, document every creative action—however small.

1. Reading a play

2. Watching a scene

3. Coaching someone

4. Taping a moment

Debrief:
You'll realize you're building more than you thought.
The waiting isn't empty—it's layered.

Exercise 2: Clock the Comparison Voice
Objective: Disarm destructive self-talk.

Any time you think, "They booked it and I didn't", pause.

Write down what you can do **right now** to strengthen your craft.

Debrief:
Replace comparison with construction.
Build instead of spiral.

Acknowledgments

This book was shaped by many voices, but forged in the quiet labor of daily teaching.

To my wife, Lorna—co-creator, companion, and witness. Your strength has kept me upright in moments when the work felt invisible. This book carries your name in every page.

To my students at *The Brownstone Class*: thank you for your hunger, your courage, your questions. You are the living proof that craft still matters.

To Dr. Aaron Adair—mentor, philosopher, friend. Your guidance helped sharpen the edges of this argument and gave it ballast. Thank you for believing in its necessity.

To the teachers whose work lit the path or forced me to forge my own:
Konstantin Stanislavsky, Stella Adler, Michael Chekhov, Sanford Meisner, Viola Spolin, Vsevolod Meyerhold, Jerzy Grotowski, Bertolt Brecht, Uta Hagen, Anne Bogart—thank you for contributing to a lineage of imagination, risk, and inquiry. Your influence can be felt in every question this book asks.

And to every actor still working in the shadows—still showing up, still searching: this book is for you.

Glossary of Terms

Actioning
The practice of identifying a specific, playable action (verb) behind each line or beat, focusing the actor's choices around pursuit rather than recitation. In this book, actioning is reclaimed as a vital, embodied tool—not a mechanical exercise.

Active Imagination
The intentional, controlled use of imagination to create detailed inner worlds, sensory environments, and emotional conditions for performance. Essential to screen acting where external stimuli may be minimal.

Adler, Stella
A renowned acting teacher and member of the Group Theatre who later broke away to champion imagination, literature, and observation over emotional memory. Influential in emphasizing the actor's relationship to the world over personal biography.

Affective Memory
A technique from early Stanislavsky, later adopted by Strasberg, in which actors recall personal emotional experiences to generate feeling on stage. Critiqued in this book as limiting and psychologically risky, especially for sustained work.

Archetypal Gesture
A concept developed by Michael Chekhov. These are symbolic, full-bodied physical gestures that express a character's core impulse, such as reaching, pushing, or protecting. Used to unlock inner life through physicality.

Behavior (in acting)
The observable physical and vocal actions of a character. Often mistaken for emotional truth in naturalistic performance. This book critiques behavior when it lacks underlying intention or stakes.

Chekhov, Michael
Nephew of Anton Chekhov and a student of Stanislavsky. Developed a method using psychological gestures and imagination to access truthful emotion through the body, rather than memory.

Consecrating Space
The actor's act of fully inhabiting a performance moment, making it sacred through complete presence, emotional risk, and truthful engagement.

Elastic Preparation
The practice of preparing multiple emotional versions of a scene to stay flexible, imaginative, and responsive, rather than locking into a single rigid interpretation.

Emotional Recall
Also called affective memory, this technique was popularized by Strasberg. Actors use personal emotional memories to trigger feelings during performance. This book critiques it for turning acting into self-reference rather than story service.

Group Theatre, The
An influential collective founded in 1931 by Harold Clurman, Cheryl Crawford, and Lee Strasberg. It brought psychological realism and naturalism to the American stage. Praised for its social consciousness, but critiqued here for mistaking stillness and authenticity for dramatic depth.

Imagination
The actor's most important creative tool. Distinguished in this book as something to be trained and exercised intentionally. Used to create detailed, truthful responses to imagined circumstances—particularly vital in screen acting.

Magic If
A core Stanislavsky tool. Asks: If I were in this character's situation, what would I do? Encourages empathy and imagination by helping actors bridge the gap between self and role.

Meaning Over Behavior
A core principle of this book: prioritizing the emotional stakes, purpose, and inner necessity behind an action rather than focusing on replicating realistic surface behavior. Acting is not about copying how people behave, but revealing what matters when they do.

Meyerhold, Vsevolod
A Russian avant-garde theatre director and contemporary of Stanislavsky. Known for developing biomechanics—a stylized physical approach to acting that emphasized rhythm, form, and movement. His work influenced Stanislavsky's later embrace of physicality and imagination.

Naturalism
An acting style emphasizing ordinary behavior and realism in surface detail. Critiqued in this book as artistically limiting when not paired with deeper dramatic stakes or interrogated meaning.

Passive Imagination
Involuntary imagination. Includes daydreams, fears, and worries. This book contrasts it with active imagination and suggests training the latter to increase an actor's adaptive range and responsiveness.

Presence
The full, conscious inhabiting of the moment by the actor, marked by emotional openness, physical responsiveness, and deep focus. Presence is not stillness or blankness; it is active availability to what is happening, internally and externally.

Psychological Gesture
Another Chekhov technique. A single, clear physical gesture that encapsulates a character's desire or emotion. Actors use it to bypass intellectual analysis and tap into embodied truth.

Realism
As defined in this book, realism is not about subtle behavior—it's about meaningful revelation. It asks not how people act, but what's at stake when they do. A realism of purpose, not just presentation.

Realism Reclaimed
The philosophy that realism in acting is not imitation or reproduction, but the interpretation of human experience through meaningful choices, contradiction, and emotional truth.

Sense Memory
A technique where actors recall sensory experiences (smell, taste, touch) to generate presence or emotional connection. Related to emotional recall but focused more on physical sensations. Used sparingly in this book's approach.

Spiritual Buoyancy
A state of emotional and imaginative resilience developed through elastic preparation. It allows the actor to remain alive, adaptive, and truthful even when conditions on set shift or collapse.

Stanislavsky's Seven Questions
A foundational tool for actor preparation:
- Who am I?
- Where am I?
- What time is it?
- What do I want?
- Why do I want it?
- What will I do to get it?
- What stands in my way?

Strasberg, Lee
Founder of the Method Acting movement in the U.S. Popularized emotional memory as the core of truthful performance. This book critiques his legacy for fostering a culture of self-mining at the expense of imagination and action.

Substitution vs. Sensation
Substitution refers to replacing a character's circumstances with personal memory (e.g., thinking about your own loss to play grief). Sensation, by contrast, builds truth through physicality, environment, and objective-driven action, allowing the character's world—not the actor's past—to lead.

About the Author

Adam Smith Jr. is an actor, teacher, and co-founder of The Brownstone Class, a screen acting workshop based in New York City. He teaches realism not as surface behavior, but as a process of discovery—through gesture, imagination, and emotional precision.

His approach draws deeply on the legacies of Adler, Chekhov, Stanislavsky, and others, but reinterprets them for a shifting screen industry where preparation must meet unpredictability. Through his classes and writing, he helps actors cultivate depth, discipline, and resilience—not just in performance, but in career and life. He lives in Hell's Kitchen with his wife, Lorna, and their miniature poodle, Doctor. *The Actor's Mirror* is his first book.